LOST RAILWAYS OF NORTH WALES

Mark Jones

COUNTRYSIDE BOOKS
NEWBURY, BERKSHIRE

First published 2008

COUNTRYSIDE BOOKS
3 Catherine Road
Newbury, Berkshire

To view our complete range of books,
please visit us at
www.countrysidebooks.co.uk

ISBN 978 1 84674 121 0

The cover picture by Colin Doggett shows the
Ffestiniog Railway; Fairlie Locomotive
Merddin Emrys in charge of an Edwardian
mixed train at Tan-y-bwlch

Designed by Peter Davies, Nautilus Design

Produced through MRM Associates Ltd., Reading
Typeset by Jean Cussons Typesetting, Diss, Norfolk
Printed by Cambridge University Press

*All material for the manufacture of this book
was sourced from sustainable forests*

CONTENTS

ACKNOWLEDGEMENTS

I would like to acknowledge all the help and support I have received in the preparation of this book. Thanks go to Gordon Suggitt and Leslie Oppitz, fellow authors in this series, for their advice and also to Leslie for sourcing and supplying many of the archive photographs used herein. Thanks also go to Chris Parker and Brian Poole for their research and planning of walks along some of the older and less accessible lines in Mid Wales, and to Phillip Earnshaw for his continued enthusiasm for our hobby and for supplying photographs. I am also grateful to my wife, Angela, for her support and advice and for tolerating my not infrequent absences from the hubbub of family life.

ABBREVIATIONS

The following abbreviations are used in this book:

CEGB	Central Electricity Generating Board
C&H	Chester & Holyhead Railway
DR&C	Denbigh, Ruthin & Corwen Railway
GC	Creat Central Railway
GWR	Great Western Railway
LMS	London, Midland & Scottish Railway
LNER	London & North Eastern Railway
LNWR	London & North Western Railway
M&M	Manchester & Milford Railway
NWMR	North Wales Mineral Railway
NWNGR	North Wales Narrow Gauge Railways
P&H	Plynlimon & Hafon Tramway
SMR	Snowdon Mountain Railway
W&L	Welsh & Llanfair Light Railway
WHLR	Welsh Highland Light Railway
WHR	Welsh Highland Railway
WM&CQ	Wrexham, Mold & Connah's Quay Railway

Introduction

North Wales, more so than anywhere else in Britain, derives a significant part of its tourist economy from its railway heritage. Though much has closed, it is reassuring to reflect on how many lines have survived. A ride on one or more of the preserved lines is, for many visitors, whether committed railway buffs or general holidaymakers, one of the highlights of their stay. Indeed, many enthusiasts build their summers around a stint as a volunteer on one or other line, contributing greatly both to the running of the lines themselves and to the local trade. However, with a little time and effort, much more of our former railway heritage can still be discovered; hopefully this book will offer some pointers in that direction.

This volume does not primarily concern itself with the railways that have survived and thrived. It aims to tell the stories of the forgotten branch lines, those that were never a viable enterprise, as well as those that served their area well for generations before becoming victims of the cutbacks of the 1950s and 1960s. It covers tramways of many types and varieties; though no book can hope to cover old tram roads comprehensively, and indeed it is quite possible in some places, armed only with a map and a sense of direction, to discover a hitherto undocumented line. It also covers some of the less well known and less conventional railways, such as the funicular lines, all with a story to tell. Starting in Anglesey, we will take a roughly circular route around North Wales.

From the urban north-east corner, with its former coal mines, to the still-pastoral vales leading down to the coast, to the more mountainous areas, many scarred by the quarrying of slate, an extensive network of railways once served the northern part of the principality. Of main lines, we now have left the former LNWR route from Chester along the northern coast to the still busy port at Holyhead, the commuter line from Wrexham to Bidston on the Wirral, the cross border route linking Wrexham with Chester and Shrewsbury, and the former Cambrian Railways route across the central belt to Aberystwyth and Pwllheli. Branches still reach Llandudno, now blessed with an hourly service from Manchester Piccadilly, and Blaenau Ffestiniog where the mountains of discarded slate waste still totally dwarf the little town and its station.

That leaves us with a multitude of lines that have not stood the test of time and it is worth spending a little while discussing, in general terms, what will have happened to them. Until quite recently, when a railway closed and the track was lifted, the formation was generally sold off piecemeal. A farmer might buy the section running through his land and infill a cutting or allow an embankment to be incorporated into a field for grazing. A householder might buy a short section to extend his garden or make an allotment. A station site might be bought and used as commercial premises, or possibly for housing, whilst a section of track near or around a town might be used to widen a road or build a new bypass. The broken trackbed in between, unable to attract a new owner, often quickly became overgrown and impassable, as it no longer served a useful purpose.

In the last twenty years or so, attitudes have gradually changed and the value of disused railways as linear routes for walking or cycling has become more generally recognised. Although railway closures are now, fortunately, rare and generally consist of freight routes no longer required for their original purpose, organisations such as the cycle path charity Sustrans are able to provide the expertise and much of the funding to enable conversions from railways to paths.

Although a number of routes, as detailed in the following chapters, are now geared up for public access, many of the sites described in this book are private and their owners do not welcome trespassers. Organisations such as the Railway Ramblers Club are able to organise visits and anyone interested in viewing such sites is advised to join one or other of the specialist societies.

A book such as this needs to set boundaries, and for this purpose the Cambrian route as far as Aberystwyth and the Mid Wales line south to Rhayader will be the furthest south we will venture. The cross border routes in the Oswestry area, including the Tanat Valley and Llanfyllin branches, have also been excluded, having been covered in the companion volume *Lost Railways of Shropshire*.

A word about place names may be of value here. When the original railway companies were preparing their proposals and parliamentary bills, many of the Welsh place names were simplified or changed to make them more easily understood by the government and legal authorities. In some cases, notably the Festiniog, the company title was not the same spelling as the place from whence it came. Many stations had anglicised versions of their place names; most of which were changed gradually to the Welsh language form over the years. The railway companies were also reluctant to use hyphenated versions of names, and many places with such titles had an amended version on their station nameboards. Such changes make consistency of names difficult; in this volume the aim has been to use the Welsh spelling unless the English version remained in use throughout the life of the station, company or line.

So, without more ado, let's get on and take a trip along the lost lines of North Wales.

Mark Jones

1
Railways of Anglesey

Main line to Holyhead
Amlwch branch
Red Wharf Bay branch
Holyhead Breakwater Railway

Llanfairpwll station, the first station in Anglesey. (Author)

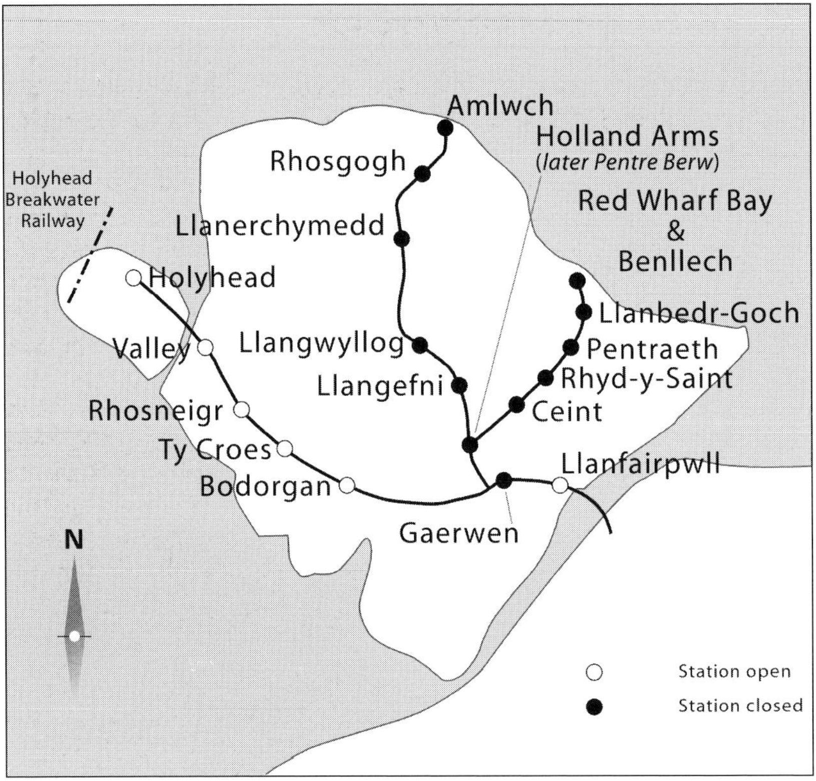

Known in Welsh as Ynys Mon, Anglesey is the largest island off the coast of either England or Wales, yet it has a relatively small population of approximately 67,000. The name Anglesey is of Viking origin, taken from *ongull* meaning 'strait' and *ey* meaning 'island', whilst 'Ynys Mon' is of Roman origin, *mon* meaning 'mother'. At one time almost exclusively Welsh-speaking, its superb beaches and quiet charming villages have attracted incomers from a wide area; to the point where Anglesey these days seems rather less 'Welsh' than many other parts of North or West Wales. Once described as the 'garden of Wales', supplying fruit and vegetables to less fertile areas, it also boasted no fewer than seventy-four parish churches, as well as the dissenting chapels so characteristic of the principality.

Main line to Holyhead

Holyhead, the chief town, has always had a different role to the rest of the island. Being the point nearest to Ireland for travellers from England and most of Wales, it developed as a port as early as the 13th century and, by the early to mid 19th century, it was busy with the business of transporting goods, mail and also many of the workmen, or navvies, required to build the numerous railways springing up across Britain. Road traffic had reached Holyhead in 1826 by means of Thomas Telford's spectacular iron bridge across the Menai Strait, a direct descendant of the original at Ironbridge.

Holyhead was therefore an early target for the railway developers, and the monopoly of the road operators lasted only a little over twenty years. The Chester & Holyhead Railway Company was formed and by March 1850 the line was completed and opened. Robert Stephenson, son of George, the famous locomotive engineer, had been entrusted with the job of designing

An engraving of Britannia Bridge by F.S. Williams. (J. Miles)

and constructing a bridge across the Menai Strait. He faced the challenge of building a very long bridge, rigid and strong enough to carry a heavy train of many carriages. This was done by constructing the bridge using two long iron tubes, rectangular in shape, through which the trains passed. This highly distinctive structure, known as the Britannia Bridge, lasted until 1970, when a ferocious fire almost completely destroyed the tubing. As Telford's road bridge was considered inadequate for the level of traffic required at that time, a decision was made to reconstruct Stephenson's bridge in double decker form. Rather than being rebuilt as a tubular bridge the new span is supported by arches. The lower deck carries a single railway track whilst the upper is now a roadway carrying traffic on the A55 expressway.

The Chester & Holyhead Railway also had high hopes of gaining the contract to carry mail across the Irish Sea, and bought four ships to serve that purpose. However, this contract was awarded to the City of Dublin Steam Packet Company and the C&H never fully recovered. By 1850, the Chester & Holyhead was leased to the LNWR, who took responsibility for operating all services and by 1859 the LNWR had fully absorbed the smaller company. Stations were opened at Llanfairpwll, Gaerwen, Bodorgan, Ty Croes, Rhosneigr and Valley, as well as Holyhead, though it was noted that these served only the more sparsely populated southern reaches of the island. Valley station eventually became very busy in its own right as a railhead for the large RAF base that was opened nearby and later also served a nuclear power station.

Some remains of the original construction of Stephenson's bridge may still be viewed. The ornamental lions on the bridge sides can be seen, though they are somewhat dwarfed by the huge road deck above. To the west of the bridge there is a section of the original iron tube, showing clearly the hollow, rectangular construction.

Somewhat bizarrely, the more famous item of railway interest remaining on Anglesey is a station nameboard. The village of Llanfairpwll or Llanfair PG lost its station in 1966 but it was reopened in 1973 for local traffic once the Britannia Bridge had been reconstructed and returned to use.

Llanfairpwllgwyngyllgogerychwyrndrobwllllantysiliogogogoch,

Llanfairpwllgwyngyllgogerychwyrndrobwllllantysiliogogogoch, without doubt the longest station nameboard in Britain. (Author)

to give it its full but rarely used name, suddenly had a claim to fame as the station with the longest name in Britain or perhaps even the world. It also sold the longest platform tickets, most of which went home as souvenirs. The station building, whilst not used for railway purposes, is still intact and in good condition.

Gaerwen, junction for the erstwhile Amlwch branch, is the only station on the main line to remain closed. The platforms have gone but the weed-strewn branch still heads north, guarded by a rusty semaphore signal. Bodorgan station building is in private hands, as is Ty Croes, where the staggered platforms are placed either side of a level crossing. At Rhosneigr a station house is privately owned and at Valley, a substantial station building on the up line is intact but boarded up. Holyhead station, rebuilt and re-sited with a glass and iron roof in 1880, was largely demolished in 1979 and replaced by smaller, modern, buildings that are considered sufficient for current needs. A ¾-mile

Holyhead station today. (Author)

extension to Holyhead Pier had closed by 1925, but a substantial bridge survives across a small inlet, now converted to road traffic use.

Amlwch branch

As early as 1852, residents of Anglesey started to complain that the new railway to Holyhead did not adequately serve the inhabitants of the island. In effect, the Chester & Holyhead Railway provided an England to Ireland service, completely missing out the main centres of population. But it was not until 1863 that a bill was passed to authorise construction of what became known as the Anglesey Central Railway. The line opened in stages from a junction with the Holyhead line at Gaerwen, first reaching the town of Llangefni in 1864. Funds for the final section to Amlwch were not easily found, and it wasn't until June 1867 that the line opened in its entirety.

As with so many locally sponsored railways, receipts did not live up to expectations, and the Anglesey Central was unable to afford its own locomotives or rolling stock, instead having to hire them from the LNWR. It did not help that the town of Amlwch failed to thrive in the mid 19th century, its population almost halving as people moved elsewhere to find work. By 1876 the local company was forced to sell the line to the LNWR for just £80,000, less than the cost of actually building it in the first place. Improvements to station buildings were carried out and passing loops installed, but there were never signal boxes, nor was there a turntable at the terminus. Passenger traffic continued somewhat uneventfully until closure following the Beeching report on 7th December 1964.

The rise and fall of freight traffic on this line is perhaps a more interesting story. In 1952 a short branch connected the line with a new chemical establishment, known originally as the 'Associated Ethyl Company' and later as 'Octel'. Raw materials produced by this company included the 'anti knocking' ingredient used in leaded petrol. Sulphur was brought into the works by rail and ethylene dibromide taken out. This provided significant business for the branch for nearly thirty years after closure to passengers; indeed, in the 1970s, it was regarded as a very busy and profitable branch but, by 1994, road transport was proving to be more cost effective, and rail traffic ceased. Earlier, further business had been obtained by transporting materials needed for the construction of an oil tank farm run by Shell to process offshore oil and send it to the huge depot at Stanlow via pipelines. A siding to this works left the Amlwch line a mile north of Rhos-goch. This site, very busy in the 1970s but now closed and with all buildings cleared, still has its sidings in place.

Since the chemical traffic ceased, the line has existed in a state of limbo for over ten years. Initial hopes that Octel or its successor, Burlington Resources Ltd, might reinstate rail traffic never materialised. In the 1990s, a company known as 'Isle of Anglesey Railways' was set up, with local council backing, aiming to reinstate a local passenger service. They succeeded in preventing the sale of the line and, after a section at Pentre Berw was lifted to allow construction of a new road bridge, it was re-laid to full specifications. However, Isle of Anglesey Railways never

Llangefni station, Amlwch branch. (Leslie Oppitz Collection)

Llangwllog station, Amlwch branch. (Leslie Oppitz Collection)

Llanerch-y-medd station, Amlwch branch. (Leslie Oppitz Collection)

Rhos-goch station, Amlwch branch. (Leslie Oppitz Collection)

Amlwch station. (Leslie Oppitz Collection)

acquired the funds to run any traffic, nor managed to purchase or lease the track and finally, in 2001, the County Council withdrew support from their scheme. A new organisation, Anglesey Central Railway, is currently attempting to raise funds to secure a lease on the line from Network Rail. However, in recent times, little has happened on the ground; the trackbed and its structures have gradually deteriorated and the prospects of any reopening for rail traffic have diminished. The Octel plant in Amlwch closed in 2003 and has since been demolished. The railway path charity Sustrans has expressed an interest in turning the line into a cycleway and footpath, and this may well be the future for this line.

It should be stressed that there is no official access to this line as it is still the property of the rail authorities, but it is reportedly intact and mostly walkable, though some stretches, particularly near Llangefni, are now overgrown and virtually impassable. Pentre Berw station, originally known as Holland Arms, the junction for the Red Wharf Bay line, was the earliest closure, in 1952, shortly after the minor branch ceased operation. The station building and yard now form part of a coal supplier's business. Llangefni station, conveniently situated for the small town at the end of High Street, is intact, together with its canopy, but is now a private residence, with much of the yard used as a car park. The next station, Llangwyllog, has also been converted to a private dwelling. At Llanerch-y-medd, both a platform and a bricked-up station building remain and can be viewed with care. Rhos-goch station is also private and has no public access anywhere near the buildings these days. At Amlwch the run-round loop and a small part of the platform are all that survive.

Red Wharf Bay branch

The Red Wharf Bay branch was a comparatively late venture by the LNWR, with an Act of Parliament passed in 1899. Even so, the company was in no hurry to build the line, starting work on it in 1907, with full opening on 24th May 1909. The aim was to take advantage of the growing tourist traffic to both the

Red Wharf Bay station in the 1920s. (Leslie Oppitz Collection)

Pentraeth station. (Leslie Oppitz Collection)

beachside camping centre at Red Wharf Bay and the slightly larger resort of Benllech. However, the branch suffered from an inexplicable decision to build the terminus some distance short of both places, with no apparent geographical explanation. Closure to passengers took place in 1930, giving only just over twenty years of use, despite the LNWR working the line from the outset using motor-train pull and push working. Freight traffic hung on until 1950. Unusually, the LNWR attempted to sell the trackbed in one lot, but apparently had it on the market for thirty-five years (presumably from just after closure to passengers) until a buyer was found who could profitably dismantle the line and then resell the trackbed.

Not a great deal remains of this line other than stretches of overgrown formation. There are minimal remains at both Ceint and Rhyd-y-saint stations, but the site of Pentraeth station was built on some years ago, with a number of houses occupying the site. Llanbedr-goch station is now incorporated into a caravan park while the terminus station site has been flattened, but is currently securely locked and not apparently being put to any use.

Holyhead Breakwater Railway

The railway built on the breakwater at Holyhead was notable for being constructed with the broad gauge that was very rarely used other than on Brunel's Great Western Railway in the south-west of England. The line, just under a mile and a half long, was constructed in this form to give a stable structure for the haulage of the very large rocks used in the base construction of the breakwater. The line was converted to standard gauge in 1912 and remained in use to carry materials for maintenance or for reconstruction after storm damage, as occurred in 1977. The line closed around 1980, latterly having being operated by one of two tiny class 01 diesel shunters. When the line closed, these unusual locomotives were unfortunately scrapped rather than offered for preservation. The southern end of the route has been converted to a footpath/cycleway. Close to the start of the actual breakwater, a small exhibition of railway relics has been put together, with the surrounding area made into a park.

Last days of the Holyhead Breakwater Railway. (Breakwater Railway Company)

Exhibition of tramway wheels and axles at the site of Holyhead Breakwater Railway. (Author)

2
The North Wales Coast Line and its Eastern Branches

Connah's Quay to Buckley
Holywell Town branch
Dyserth branch
Llandudno Junction to Llandudno
Great Orme Tramway and other railways in Llandudno
Foryd Pier and Kinmel Camp

Llandudno Junction in its heyday. (Lens of Sutton)

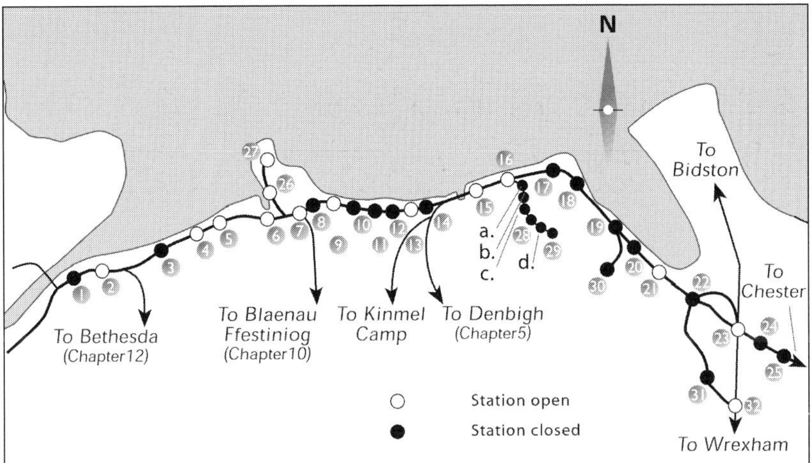

1. Menai Bridge
2. Bangor
3. Aber
4. Llanfairfechan
5. Penmaenmawr
6. Conwy
7. Llandudno Junction
8. Mochdre & Pabo
9. Colwyn Bay
10. Old Colwyn
11. Llysfaen
12. Llandulas
13. Abergele & Pensarn
14. Foryd
15. Rhyl
16. Prestatyn
a. Chapel Street Halt
b. Woodland Park Halt
c. St Melyd Golf Links Halt
d. Allt-y-Graig Halt
17. Talacre
18. Mostyn
19. Holywell Junction
20. Bagillt
21. Flint
22. Connah's Quay
23. Shotton
24. Queensferry
25. Sandycroft
26. Deganwy
27. Llandudno
28. Meliden
29. Dyserth
30. Holywell Town
31. Buckley
32. Buckley Junction

As discussed in Chapter 1, the primary reason for early development of the North Wales Coast line was to secure a contract for the Irish Mail. Holyhead had lost the mail service in 1839 to Liverpool, following the completion of a rail link from London, but given the much greater speed and safety of land transport over sea, this was never considered a fully satisfactory arrangement. Proposals to construct a rail terminal and port at Ormes Bay near Llandudno were considered, but the mail bosses wanted the sea crossing to be as short as possible. In 1840 a government committee approved the coastal route to Holyhead, and the necessary parliamentary procedures were completed by 1844. The line from Chester to Bangor, a fraction short of 60 miles in length, opened on 1st May 1848, with the first Holyhead to Euston express running on 18th March 1850.

The LNWR soon started to look at the possibility of tourist traffic; the first resort to develop being Rhyl, where a pier, winter gardens and many hotels were built for the discerning visitor. Rhyl was closely followed by Colwyn Bay and, most successfully, by Llandudno. Rail traffic continued to grow throughout the 19th century. Stations opened in 1848/49 at Queensferry, Bagillt, Holywell (later Holywell Junction), Mostyn, Prestatyn, Colwyn Bay, Penmaenmawr and Aber were joined by Britannia Bridge in 1851 (closed in 1858), Menai Bridge in 1858, Llanfairfechan in 1860 and Llandulas (later renamed Llysfaen) in 1862. Further stations were built later on at Connah's Quay, Sandycroft, Old Colwyn, Foryd, Mochdre & Pabo, Talacre and Shotton. In 1889 a new

Bagillt station, with platforms serving only the slower pair of the four tracks. (Lens of Sutton)

The exterior of Mostyn station today. (Author)

A current view of Mostyn station shed. (Author)

station was built at Llandulas (a mile to the east of the previous one, which then became Llysfaen). Quadrupling of much of the line east of Llandudno Junction had taken place by the First World War.

The North Wales Coast line was also notable for its pioneering use of water troughs to allow locomotives to take on water on the move and thus allow non-stop running over greater distances. Troughs opened near Mochdre in 1860 before being moved to Aber in 1871, with further examples installed west of Prestatyn and south-east of Flint. These remained in use until the final demise of regular steam-hauled traffic in the 1960s.

Tourism and its associated traffic continued to develop well into the 20th century, but the focus gradually drifted down-market from grand hotels with immaculate bowling greens and genteel reading rooms to more down-to-earth caravan and camping sites. In 1939 a holiday camp was opened in Prestatyn as a joint venture between Thomas Cook and the LMS. It was later taken over by Pontins and, though used for military purposes by the Royal Signallers during the Second World War, became an extremely popular destination from the 1940s onwards.

A post war view of Conwy (Conway) station. (Leslie Oppitz Collection)

Not every location along the north coast thrived, and closure of the least-used stations started in the 1930s. Llysfaen, Foryd (re-opened in 1938 as Kinmel Bay Halt) and Mochdre & Pabo closed in 1931 with Llandulas and Old Colwyn following in 1952. The rationalisation of the 1960s started with closures of Aber (1960) and Sandycroft (1961) stations, followed by removal of much of the quadrupling. Closure of lesser-used stations continued in 1966, which saw the demise of Queensferry, Shotton (reopened 1972), Connah's Quay, Bagillt, Holywell Junction, Mostyn, Talacre, Conway (reopened as Conwy in 1987) and Menai Bridge. Of these, Mostyn station is perhaps the best preserved, with a very fine station building (private) and a two-track shed still standing.

With mile upon mile of caravans cluttering the coastal fringe and the A55 dual carriageway almost alongside, it cannot be denied that today's rail journey along the North Wales coast is less attractive than it once was. However, its future seems secure now, and for that we should be grateful.

Connah's Quay to Buckley

Originally known as the Buckley Railway, but later part of the Great Central's portfolio of railways in north-east Wales, this line opened in 1862, primarily to serve collieries in the area to the north and west of Buckley. A number of small quarries and brickworks were also served but no regular passenger service ever existed. It is thought that much of the line was built on the trackbed of some old narrow gauge tramways but little evidence of these lines remains. The Buckley Railway required gradients as steep as 1 in 30 to take the line down to the coast at Connah's Quay. Largely duplicated by the line from Wrexham to Hawarden Bridge and the Wirral, which passed a mile or so to the east of Buckley, the section as far south as Northop Hall closed in 1959, with the section through the centre of Buckley to Buckley Junction following in 1965. The northernmost part through Connah's Quay was quickly built over by housing and only small, isolated sections remain of the line through Northop Hall and Buckley.

Buckley Junction, terminus of the branch from Connah's Quay. Now renamed Buckley, it is these days a mere halt on the Wrexham to Bidston line. (Lens of Sutton)

The final section to Buckley Junction was converted into a public footpath.

Holywell Town branch

The original Holywell station on the Chester & Holyhead line could hardly have been more inconvenient for the small town it was supposed to serve. As well as being over 1½ miles from the centre of Holywell, it was also over 500 ft lower, the town being situated on the heights of Halkyn Mountain. Lead mining and copper smelting were long-standing industries in Holywell, and an early 3 ft gauge tramway was built to take these materials down to a wharf on the River Dee at Greenfield. This tramway crossed the Chester & Holyhead line on the level south-east of the main line station. By the mid 19th century the tramway was considered inadequate and in 1864 an Act was passed which authorised the construction of a standard gauge line on the original tramway alignment. This included a connecting line to the Chester & Holyhead line, a new pier at Greenfield and the replacement of the level crossing at Greenfield by a bridge. However, the new mineral line had an effective working life of only four years, its construction unfortunately coinciding with a major downturn in industrial activity further up the valley. By 1874 the line was derelict, and it remained in this state for over thirty years, despite being bought by the LNWR in 1891. Not until 1912 did the LNWR open the line to passengers, having previously considered and discounted an electric tramway.

The height difference over a relatively short distance necessitated extremely steep gradients, mostly of 1 in 27, with Holywell Town station itself built on a gradient of 1 in 51. The LNWR provided a quite intensive service, with more than sixteen trains per day running at one stage, but eventually competition from buses led to closure in 1954. A small section at the northern end survived a further three years for freight.

Holywell Town station, showing the severe downward gradient that commenced immediately after the end of the platform. (Leslie Oppitz Collection)

Having been used unofficially by the public for many years, the line was purchased by the local council in 1974 and officially designated a footpath five years later. The trackbed can now be walked for virtually its whole route. Holywell Town station, situated in a large, man-made hollow, was landscaped and has no obvious railway remnants other than the top of a retaining wall in the goods yard. The platform has apparently not been destroyed; instead it is believed to be lying intact under tons of earth. The site of the intermediate halt at St Winifrides (to serve the famous well) is marked only by a local authority sign, and the ruins of Basingwerk Abbey, close by, may also be seen. The Grade II listed station building at Holywell Junction, at one time in poor condition, has recently been restored and converted to a very fine private residence.

Dyserth branch

The Dyserth branch, built by the LNWR to serve lead and haematite mines in the upper Prestatyn Valley, opened in 1869. Passenger services were developed in the early 20th century, starting in 1905, more for the benefit of the tourist traffic to the waterfalls at Cwm and the ruined castle at Dyserth than for the local inhabitants. Services left from a now overgrown bay platform on the west side of Prestatyn station and had to reverse before accessing the branch. A number of ground level halts were introduced to increase traffic, but the passenger service was an early casualty, closing in 1930. Freight traffic from Dyserth quarry and from a number of mills along the valley kept the branch in operation until 1973, after which attempts were made to reopen it as a preserved line. To this end Rhuddlan Council bought the trackbed in 1983, but eventually the preservation plan foundered and the branch was converted to a footpath in 1990.

As the line was purchased in its entirety, it is walkable virtually the whole way, from a crossing just south of Prestatyn station right through to Dyserth. At Meliden both a stone goods shed and a part of a loading gauge survives, and while some railway buildings at Dyserth remain, they are now in commercial use and not really recognisable as such. Just to the east of Dyserth station lies a rare example of walkable trackbed that was never laid with track. A light railway extension from Dyserth was authorised in both 1908 and 1915 to serve Marian Mills, forming the first part of a proposed route to Trelawynd. To encourage the LNWR to complete this route, a local landowner, Mr Pochin, built a section of about ¾ mile on his own land and at his own expense. However, the First World War put an end to this development

Prestatyn station today. One pair of lines has long since been removed, whilst the Dyserth branch ran from the overgrown bay platform behind the nameboard. (Author)

Dyserth branch, a goods shed survives at Meliden. (Author)

and Mr Pochin's formation remained forever isolated and unused. Public access to this unusual remnant is still permitted.

Llandudno Junction to Llandudno

Llandudno soon proved to be the most popular of the developing resorts on the North Wales coast, beautifully situated with two fine bays below the lofty heights of the Great Orme. Despite not being served by the Chester & Holyhead, hotels and boarding houses quickly sprung up at a site that was, as late as 1849, boasting little more than two inns and a few scattered cottages. A three-mile branch opened in 1858, and the success of the line was shown by the need for doubling, which took place in 1875, and by development of both the terminus station and Llandudno Junction, which was rebuilt and extended in 1897. A short branch ran south from Deganwy, the line's one intermediate station, to serve a wharf which facilitated the movement of timber and slate out of the Conwy Valley, narrow gauge quarry trucks being carried on specially adapted standard gauge wagons. This line opened in 1885 and remained in use until the 1930s.

Deganwy station, Llandudno branch, today. Little remains except the fine footbridge. (Author)

A 1980s' view of Llandudno station. (Phillip Earnshaw)

Great Orme Tramway and other railways in Llandudno

The Great Orme line was promoted as much as a tourist attraction in Llandudno than as a convenient means of transport to get people up to the top of the Great Orme. Having been promoted under a light railway order by the Great Orme Tramways Act of 1898, construction began in 1901, with the route opening for passengers in stages from July 1902 to 1903.

The line is effectively split into two, with passengers having to change cars at the Halfway station. Starting at what is known as the Victoria station on Church Walks, the lower section climbs 400 ft in around half a mile at gradients of up to 1 in 4 up Old Road and then via Black Gate and Ty Gwyn Road to the Halfway station. Here, there is a winding house, powered by steam until conversion to electrical operation in the 1950s. The upper section is less steep and climbs 150 ft in about the same distance. Having changed ownership in the 1930s, the tramway remained in private hands until 1949 when Llandudno Urban District Council bought it under powers to compulsorily purchase the undertaking at seven-yearly intervals. The line has remained publicly owned ever since and is now run under the auspices of Conwy County Council.

Between 1951 and 1953 there was briefly a second railway on the Great Orme, when a single track miniature railway of 10¼ inch gauge was constructed about 400 yards long on a plateau

Great Orme Tramway, Llandudno. Car No 5 at Victoria station. (Author)

just below the summit. This tiny railway was rumoured to have been owned and promoted by the boxer, Randolph Turpin.

Mention should also be made of the 3 ft 6 inch gauge Llandudno & Colwyn Bay Electric Railway, which operated from October 1907 to March 1956 between those two towns. Despite its name, this was a conventional street-running electric tramway, indeed the last privately-owned street tramway to remain in use anywhere in Britain. After trams were replaced by buses, all traces were gradually obliterated.

Foryd Pier and Kinmel Camp Railway

A continuation north of the Vale of Clwyd line from Denbigh to Foryd reached Foryd Pier by 1859, but although a station was built at the terminus in 1865, a regular passenger service never materialised. Freight continued to serve this ¾ mile branch until April 1959. South of Foryd, a single track line, just under 3 miles long, served a military camp at Kinmel, near Kinmel Hall. At its busiest during the First World War, the line continued in operation, latterly diesel operated, to serve local quarries until 1964. The Kinmel Camp line remains walkable as a somewhat uneventful public right of way for much of its length across the plain east of Abergele, from Towyn as far south as the modern A55 dual carriageway.

3
Wrexham Area

North Wales Mineral Railway
Wrexham to Brymbo (GWR)
Wrexham to Moss
Wrexham to Buckley, Shotton and Connah's Quay (WM&CQ)
Wrexham to Brymbo (WM&CQ)
Wrexham to Rhos
Brymbo to Ffrith junction and Mold

A smartly staffed Brymbo station in passenger days. (Lens of Sutton)

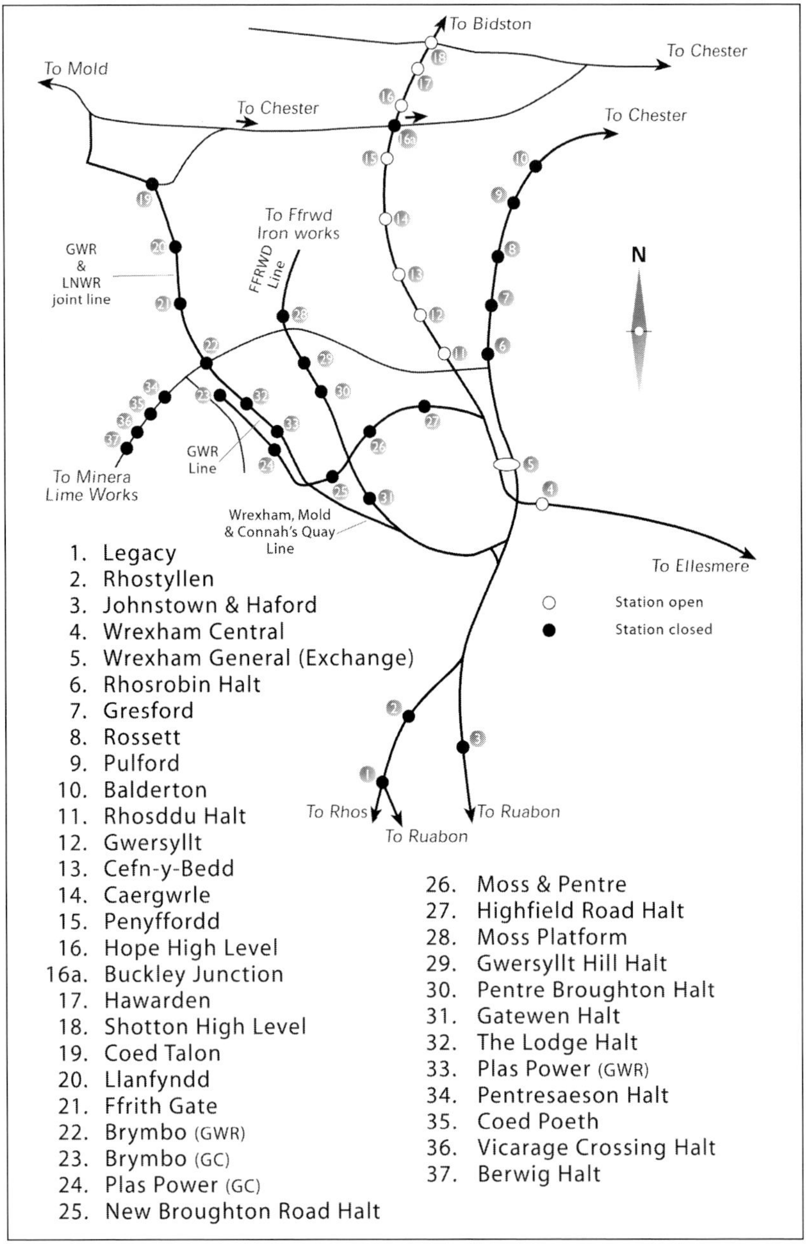
To Bidston
To Chester
To Mold
To Chester
To Chester
To Ffrwd
Iron works
FFRWD
Line
GWR
&
LNWR
joint line
N
GWR
Line
To Minera
Lime Works
Wrexham, Mold
& Connah's Quay
Line
To Ellesmere
Station open
Station closed
To Rhos
To Ruabon
To Ruabon
1. Legacy
2. Rhostyllen
3. Johnstown & Haford
4. Wrexham Central
5. Wrexham General (Exchange)
6. Rhosrobin Halt
7. Gresford
8. Rossett
9. Pulford
10. Balderton
11. Rhosddu Halt
12. Gwersyllt
13. Cefn-y-Bedd
14. Caergwrle
15. Penyffordd
16. Hope High Level
16a. Buckley Junction
17. Hawarden
18. Shotton High Level
19. Coed Talon
20. Llanfyndd
21. Ffrith Gate
22. Brymbo (GWR)
23. Brymbo (GC)
24. Plas Power (GC)
25. New Broughton Road Halt
26. Moss & Pentre
27. Highfield Road Halt
28. Moss Platform
29. Gwersyllt Hill Halt
30. Pentre Broughton Halt
31. Gatewen Halt
32. The Lodge Halt
33. Plas Power (GWR)
34. Pentresaeson Halt
35. Coed Poeth
36. Vicarage Crossing Halt
37. Berwig Halt

Anyone who looks at a British railway atlas dating from any time prior to the 1980s will realise that former coal mining districts always seemed to have the most comprehensive network of lines. The area around Wrexham was especially complex and, in addition to the collieries, there were ironworks, particularly at Bersham and Brymbo, which acted as a magnet (no pun intended!) to the railway companies. A canal branch to link with the waterways network at Chester was at one time planned but never materialised. The former GWR line from Chester to Shrewsbury crosses into Wales for some distance north of Wrexham and south of Ruabon, but has been amply covered in the companion volume *Lost Railways of Cheshire*.

North Wales Mineral Railway

Heading west from Wheatsheaf junction to the north of Wrexham, the main line of the North Wales Mineral Railway (NWMR) had reached a lime works at Minera, west of Brymbo, a distance of just over 6 miles, by July 1847. Running laterally across the valleys, the line required two tunnels, one of 220 yards at Summer Hill near Gwersyllt, and one of 400 yards at Brymbo. Even more inconveniently, to climb up the sides of the valleys, two rope-worked inclines had to be constructed, one near Gwersyllt and one at Moss just to the east of Brymbo Tunnel. The two inclines were known locally as 'brakes' and this term was commemorated when in 1885 a chapel built at Moss was named the 'Brake Methodist Church'. Branches, both just over one mile in length were constructed from Brymbo to Vron Colliery and from Moss to Ffrwd via Westminster Colliery. Both these branches opened in November 1847, and a short spur to Gwersyllt Colliery was added at around the same time.

By September 1854 the NWMR had become the property of the GWR and, given the rapidly increasing traffic on the line, a solution had to be found to overcome the bottlenecks caused by the inclines. The answer was to build a line from south of Wrexham, branching off the Ruabon line then via Croes Newydd to Brymbo (see below). This made redundant the section east of

Brymbo, including Brymbo Tunnel and the adjacent incline, but much of the rest of the NWMR continued to be profitable and busy for many years. The next stretch to close, in October 1908, was the section between the junction with the spur to Gwersyllt Colliery, via the second incline and Summer Hill Tunnel, and Moss, where a later line up the Moss Valley (see below), could serve the collieries and ironworks to the north of this point. Westminster Colliery to Ffos-y-go (Ffrwd) closed in 1917, followed by the stub to Westminster Colliery itself, in 1925, and that to Vron Colliery in 1930. Wheatsheaf junction to Gwersyllt Colliery lasted until 1951, and the westernmost and originally the most isolated section of line, from Brymbo to Minera Lime Works, lasted until January 1972. A passenger service using railmotors operated on part of the western section of the NWMR between 1905 and 1930; this is discussed in the section on the GWR's Wrexham to Brymbo route.

The eastern end of the NWMR was largely obliterated, either by landscaping of the valleys or by housing development. However, the Summer Hill incline is a remarkable, if isolated, survivor; it can still be seen as a grassy footpath, partly on a slight embankment, running between rows of houses. In 1984 the nearby entrance to Summer Hill Tunnel could also still be viewed, with '1847' inscribed on the stonework above.

Wrexham to Brymbo (GWR)

Due to the high volume of steel being produced at the Brymbo works, the GWR needed to provide a quicker and more efficient route for this traffic. As a result, a new line from Croes Newydd, south of Wrexham, incorporating a triangular junction that allowed traffic to reach the new line from the south or the north, was opened in May 1862. Built as double track throughout, in clear anticipation of the traffic demands, a passenger service from Wrexham to Brymbo commenced in May 1882. An intermediate station was provided at Plas Power the following year. This proved successful and the GWR decided to extend the service to Coed Poeth, via a somewhat indirect route from Wrexham, on the

Brymbo (GWR) station after closure. (Leslie Oppitz Collection)

NWMR's Minera Extension. The new service commenced in November 1897 and was further extended to Berwig Halt in May 1905; a rare example of a passenger service terminating at a halt.

After steam railmotors took over operation, further halts were provided at Brymbo West Crossing, Pentresaeson and Vicarage Crossing (east of Berwig), with the last to open being 'The Lodge' on the southern side of Brymbo, first appearing on the timetable in July 1906. This service continued until January 1931 when it closed alongside a number of other similar services operated by the GWR in the area, who at that time were heavily promoting bus services for small volume, short-distance commuter traffic. Freight traffic continued to Brymbo long enough for a bridge to be provided for the line to pass under the Wrexham bypass, but all traffic north of Moss Valley junction had ceased to run by 1983.

Wrexham to Moss

The degree of development of coal and mineral extraction, combined with the associated increase in the population of the area, led the GWR to construct a further line up into the Moss Valley, where it was to compete with the earlier Wrexham, Mold & Connah's Quay Railway (see below). Opened in May 1882, this

The Wrexham to Moss line is now a cycleway for most of its length, linking the town with Moss Valley Park. (Author)

line enabled the GWR to reach Ffrwd Ironworks and also serve collieries at Caepenty, Brynmally, Westminster (originally via the NWMR) and Gatewen. A passenger service, operated from the start by railmotors, running as far as Moss Platform, started in May 1905. Intermediate halts were opened at Gwersyllt Hill (1906), Pentre Broughton and Gatewen (1908). This service proved even less profitable than the route to Berwig via Brymbo, but struggled along until both lines shut in January 1931. By this time the collieries in the Moss Valley had been more or less worked out, and the line closed, apparently for good in 1935, though, for some reason the rails remained *in situ* for many years and were not lifted until 1952.

A limited revival for the Moss Valley line took place in the 1970s. Firstly, tracks were re-laid as far as the site of Gatewen Colliery, which at the time was serving as a railhead for extensive opencast works in the area. A further extension opened when track was reinstated for another half mile, close to the former site of Pentre Broughton Halt, where a rail delivery depot was constructed. This spur continued in operation until 1991. Much of this route has now been converted to a cycleway, which links the outskirts of Wrexham with Moss Valley Park.

Wrexham to Buckley, Shotton and Connah's Quay (Wrexham, Mold & Connah's Quay Railway)

In contrast to the great majority of the local railway companies in North Wales, the Wrexham, Mold & Connah's Quay Railway

(WM&CQ) survived as an independent concern as late as the 1890s, when it overstretched itself, unable to fund the construction of lines it was building from Shotton to Bidston and from Dee Marsh junction to Chester. Taken over by the Great Central in 1897, the WM&CQ was therefore transferred to the LNER at grouping (1923), becoming very much an isolated outpost of that company's operations.

The line to link Wrexham with the Buckley line, and hence the docks at Connah's Quay, was authorised by an Act of 1862, with opening to goods in January 1866 and passengers the same year. A terminus was built adjacent to the GWR's Wrexham General station. At first, the only intermediate stations were Gwersyllt & Wheatsheaf (later Gwersyllt), Cefn-y-bedd and Hope (originally Caergwle, then Hope Village), but further stations were added at Penyffordd (1877) and Caergwle (1872, originally Bridge End, later Caergwle Castle). South of Brymbo junction a halt was constructed at Rhosddu, but this was purely for the Brymbo service and only operated between 1906 and 1917. After construction of the route to Shotton and the Wirral, the Buckley line declined rapidly in importance but hung on as a through route for freight between Wrexham and the North Wales coast until 1962. Part of a stub to Northop Hall continued in use until 1965; this one-mile stretch was an early conversion to an official public footpath.

The 'new' line, opened in 1890 between Buckley Junction and Shotton, can be considered both a success and a failure. A success because it remains busy to this day; part of the commuter system linking Wrexham and north-east Wales with Liverpool and the Wirral, with rumours and plans for electrification often filling the pages of the railway press. To the WM&CQ, however, it was a failure as construction helped virtually bankrupt the independent line and led to its sale to the Great Central. Just prior to the opening of the Hawarden line there was expansion southwards, where in 1887 a new station, appropriately named Wrexham Central, was constructed closer to the town where it later formed an end-on junction with the Wrexham & Ellesmere Railway (see *Lost Railways of Shropshire*). Wrexham Central, impressive in its day, declined in importance after the Ellesmere line closed and eventually was reduced to a single platform with no substantial

Wrexham Central, before closure of the line (far right) to Ellesmere. (Lens of Sutton)

The last days of the original Wrexham Central, reduced to a single platform and a 'bus shelter'. (Phillip Earnshaw)

buildings at all. In recent years it has been replaced by a modern structure a few hundred yards to the west, with the original site built over with retail units.

Between 1891 and 1967, a short branch curved north-west from a junction just north of Shotton station to reach the dock rea at Connah's Quay near to the east of the Buckley Railway's route.

The new Wrexham Central today, a few hundred yards to the west of the original. (Author)

Wrexham to Brymbo (Wrexham, Mold & Connah's Quay Railway)

The Wrexham, Mold & Connah's Quay Railway did not by any means have things all its own way in the Wrexham area, competing with both the LNWR who ran the lines from Mold and Ffrith junction to Brymbo via Coed Talon, but more significantly with the GWR. A look at the relevant page of a railway atlas shows all three companies in fierce competition, not only serving the same collieries and mineral works, but actually duplicating each other's routes and running alongside each other in places.

Having opened their line from Connah's Quay to Wrexham by 1866 (the WM&CQ never got anywhere near Mold), the smaller company was able at the same time to commence reaching the Moss Valley and Ffrwd Ironworks via a line running north from Ffrwd junction. The southernmost section, to Ffos-y-go, closed in

Cefn-y-bedd station, north of Wrexham on the Bidston line, with its distinctive waiting shelter intact. (Author)

1912, the ironworks ceased to require traffic from 1930 and the final section, to Brynmally Colliery, ceased to operate in 1935.

The second line into the Wrexham coalfield operated by the WM&CQ was perhaps the more interesting, particularly as it briefly operated a passenger service. Running south-west from the triangular Brymbo junction, a couple of miles to the north of Wrexham, the line opened in stages, reaching a terminus at Brymbo by an indirect 'U' shaped route. Short spurs reached Gatewen and Vron collieries, both already served by the GWR, while a minor branch reached a new railhead at Plas Power. A passenger service opened in January 1889, but this seemed doomed from the outset; the line had a direct competitor, it missed the main villages, and it had a mileage twice that of the local direct route buses. Intermediate halts were provided at Plas Power and Moss & Pentre, with two others, Highfield Road and New Broughton Road, neither close to any centres of population, appearing on the timetable in 1905. It was only the pride of the relatively new Great Central, who didn't want to give an impression of failure to its rivals, as might be indicated by closing lines, which kept the line going. However, economies were required and the passenger service to Brymbo (WM&CQ) station ceased in March 1917.

The line continued to be busy into nationalisation days, though Brymbo South junction to Brymbo West junction had closed in 1925. In November 1954 a junction was made with the ex-GWR line near Brymbo and this enabled some duplicate lines to be eliminated. The last section to close, in October 1970, was that to Vron Colliery via the goods terminus at Brymbo.

Wrexham to Rhos

As Wrexham developed as an administrative and commercial centre for north-east Wales and Ruabon declined in importance, the GWR felt it worthwhile to construct a line between Rhosllanerchrugog (Rhos) and Wrexham. Branching south-west from Rhos junction, a mile or so south of Wrexham, the line opened to freight in October 1901 and to passengers in March 1905. An intermediate station was provided at Rhostyllen and a halt at Legacy, which also served for a while as the terminus of a railmotor service on the Ponkey branch from Ruabon (see Chapter 4). Legacy had a classic 'pagoda shaped' wooden shelter on its platform, similar to many built by the GWR in its heartland further south.

Busy with coal and brickwork traffic, the line continued to serve the locality for these purposes until October 1963. The Wrexham to Rhos passenger service was well used for a while but, being short in distance and parallel to the main road, the area was better served by buses. Regular services ceased in January 1931, though excursion trains to Wrexham FC home matches continued to the mid 1950s and many special trains reached Rhos from all parts of Wales for the National Eisteddfod held there in August 1945. Much of the northern part of this line was obliterated by the building of the Wrexham bypass in the 1970s.

Brymbo to Ffrith junction and Mold

From Ffrith junction, the LNWR's steeply graded Ffrith Railway opened in 1849 and ran for just under 4 miles through Coed Talon to Llanfynydd where an end on junction was made with the LNWR and GWR joint line to Brymbo. This line opened in 1872, making the LNWR become the second of three companies to gain access to the steelworks there. Meanwhile a single-track line opened in July 1870 from Tryddyn junction, just east of Mold, to Coed Talon where a triangular junction was formed with the Ffrith line. At some stage in the later years of the 19th century this

Coed Talon station, Mold to Brymbo line, after abandonment of the north and east sides of the triangular junction. (Leslie Oppitz Collection)

Ffrith station, after closure, on the occasion of a 1950 railtour. (Leslie Oppitz Collection)

section must have fallen into disuse, as preparations for its opening to passengers in 1891 refer to 'works to enable the line to reopen'. A somewhat sparse service of three to four trains each way per day between Mold and Wrexham via Brymbo operated from January 1892 with an intermediate station at Coed Talon. Further stations followed at Llanfynydd and Ffrith in 1898.

The section south from Ffrith junction was the first to be made 'surplus to requirements', closing in 1934 along with the north and east sides of the triangle at Coed Talon. Closure to passengers of the Mold to Brymbo route followed in March 1950, and then complete closure took place in stages as the mines and yards served gradually closed, with the final section north of Brymbo to Bwlchgwyn Siding ceasing operation in October 1963. This line is not walkable, but a fine though inaccessible viaduct still strides across the valley to the west of Ffrith.

A viaduct at Ffrith still strides across the village. (Author)

4
Ruabon Area

Ruabon to Llangollen
Ruabon to Legacy (Ponkey branch)
Rhos to Pontcysyllte and Trevor
(Ruabon Brook Tramway)
Ruabon to Plas Madoc and Acrefair

Ruabon station in the 1960s, at that time still a junction for Llangollen and the Bala line. (Lens of Sutton)

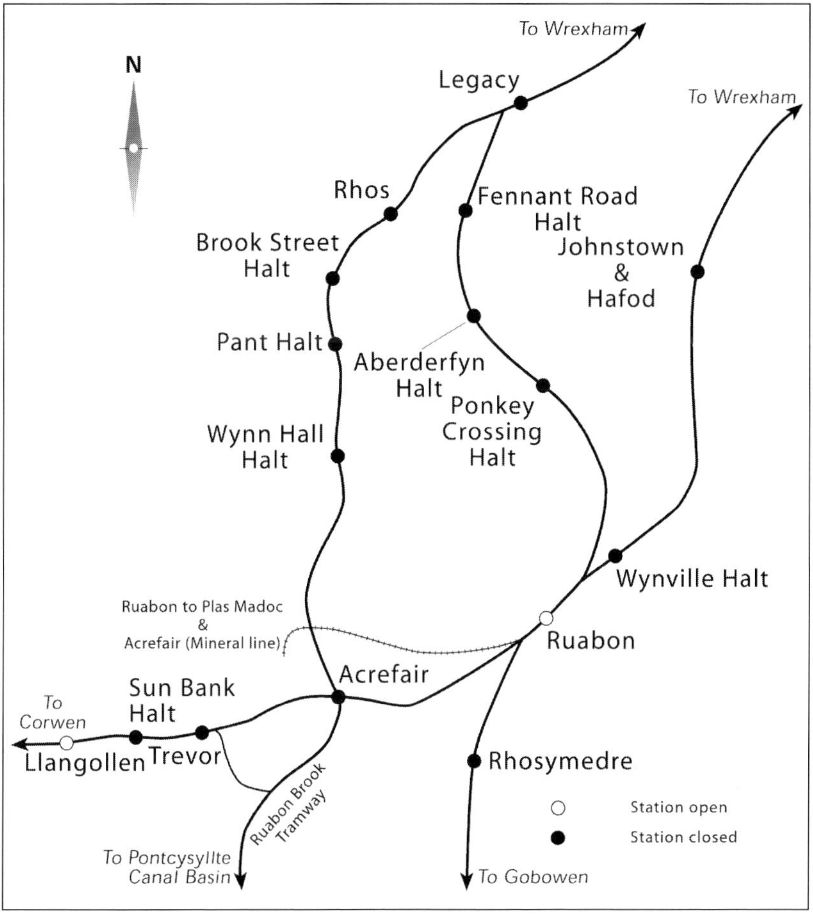

Ruabon to Llangollen

Llangollen was an early tourist destination and as such a target for many of the local railway promoters; the Vale of Llangollen Railway being the one who eventually won the battle to build a line from Ruabon. Whilst the local company had modest aspirations, they were backed by the GWR whose intentions, even as early as the late 1850s, were to use the line as a staging post to reach the Mid Wales coast. The GWR also had their eye on the

Ruabon station in 2005, showing the overgrown Llangollen bay platform to the right. (Author)

The footbridge at Ruabon no longer gives access to the far platform! (Author)

Llangollen station before closure in the 1960s. (Lens of Sutton)

A modern view of Llangollen station, showing its beautiful riverside location. (Author)

Vale of Clwyd line (see Chapter 5) and had negotiations ended differently might well have seen them reach Rhyl and the north coast as well.

The line to Llangollen was authorised by an Act of 1859, with opening to freight in December 1861 and passengers in June 1862. Intermediate stations were provided at Acrefair and Trevor. The line was doubled from Ruabon junction to Llangollen Goods junction, ½ mile west of Llangollen, in September 1900. Acrefair, Trevor and Llangollen stations were remodelled, and an extra stop at Garth & Sun Bank Halt (Sun Bank Halt from 1906) opened in 1905. This was the site of an accident in September 1945 where flooding from the canal, which runs parallel to and slightly above the railway at this point, completely washed away a whole section of trackbed and embankment. A freight and mail train fell into the resulting chasm, leading to the loss of life of the driver. Sun Bank Halt ceased to appear in the timetable in June 1950, later followed by closure of the whole line to passengers in January 1965 and total closure in April 1968.

Ruabon station became an unstaffed halt in 1974, though the main station building and part of the original footbridge remain.

The end of the line at Llangollen. Will the tracks ever reach Ruabon again? (Author)

The bay platform is intact but heavily overgrown after 40 years of disuse. Nothing remains to be seen at Acrefair, though a partially infilled deep cutting to the south of the station site may still be viewed. At Trevor, the industrial belt around Ruabon ceases and the line enters open countryside. Here it is still possible to view the remains of two lengthy platforms, together with steps down to the former station building and the foundations of the old signalbox. West of Trevor the formation is intact, but is in private hands and not officially accessible. The course of the line running through the eastern outskirts of Llangollen has largely been built on, and efforts to keep a space for a single track should restoration become possible appear to have been in vain. (Llangollen station is now open again as part of the preserved railway westwards – see Chapter 6, Llangollen Railway section.)

Ruabon to Legacy (Ponkey branch)

Ponkey seems a most peculiar name in English, but is, in fact, merely an anglicisation of 'Ponciau', meaning small hillock. By the mid 19th century furnaces had been developed at this location and at Aberderfyn slightly further north, where there was also a gasworks. In August 1861 the GWR opened what was then termed a siding from Gardden Lodge junction, just north-east of Ruabon, to serve these works, and in August 1876 built a continuation to Legacy, eventually forming a junction with the later line from Wrexham to Rhos, a mile or so north of the latter.

In the early part of the 20th century the GWR believed that they could profitably operate passenger services on minor lines such as this using railmotors, and accordingly from June 1905 started a service south from Legacy, with halts at Fennant Road, Aberderfyn and Ponkey Crossing. However, passenger trains were to last less than ten years, as the GWR did not have sufficient resources to run these types of services during the First World War, and the service ceased in March 1915. As none of the freight traffic headed northwards towards Wrexham, the line was severed in 1917 between Legacy, where a short section was retained as a siding, and Aberderfyn. Further goods facilities were installed at Moreton, for petrol and at the Ruabon Brick and Terra Cotta Company, keeping the line busy until the 1950s. Closure was in two stages, with the section north of the brick company to Aberderfyn closing in October 1954 and the final stub to the brickworks seeing its last train in August 1964. Virtually all this line was built over in the years after closure.

Rhos to Pontcysyllte and Trevor (Ruabon Brook Tramway)

The Ruabon Brook Tramway had a somewhat complex history, which reflected its gradual change in role from a canal-feeding tramroad to a minor but useful part of the national rail network. Originally constructed by the Ellesmere Canal Company in 1805, its purpose was to bring stone down from stone quarries at Cefn to the canal at Pontcysyllte. It is worth noting that only in comparatively recent times has the canal been known as the 'Llangollen', being originally merely a navigable feeder to the Pontcysyllte arm of the Ellesmere Canal. This in turn became incorporated into the Shropshire Union Canal, terminating at the

Ruabon Brook Tramway; embankment north of Pontcysyllte. (Author)

Tiny wagons used to pass under this bridge to reach the canal basin at Pontcysyllte. (Author)

'port for Ellesmere', which eventually became known as Ellesmere Port.

Returning to the tramway, this quickly proved successful and was extended in 1808 to serve a small colliery at Plas Madoc, and later via various other collieries and brickworks to a point a mile or so south of Rhosllanerchrugog (Rhos). Conversion to a railway took place in stages, during the 1860s, in some places with a slight diversionary route, and did not require an Act of Parliament as the land was bought privately, with an extension to Rhos opening in January 1867. The tramway passed under the Ruabon to Llangollen line just to the west of Acrefair station. After being purchased by the GWR in 1896, further spurs were added, firstly north of Rhos to Legacy, linking with the Ponkey branch and then eastwards towards Wrexham. At the same time a short spur was constructed to the eastern end of Trevor station, which gave access to Llangollen and points further west.

A railmotor service operated south to a halt at Wynn Hall, close to the colliery of that name, from March 1905 to March 1915 with intermediate stops south of Rhos at Brook Street and Pant. The southernmost section of the route, from Pontcysyllte to Pant, was the first to close, in 1953, though rail/canal interchange at Pontcysyllte had ceased around 1919. Pant to Rhos closed in October 1963 and the spur from Trevor survived the longest, supplying a chemical works until January 1968.

The most notable remnant these days is a large stretch of overgrown brick-arched embankment running parallel to the road leading north out of Pontcysyllte, together with a couple of bridge abutments, and an arch under a minor road close to the old canal basin under which tiny wagons were once hauled. The explorer of old lines will find almost nothing these days in Acrefair or points further north, other than a short stretch incorporated into a public footpath south of Pant.

Ruabon to Plas Madoc and Acrefair

This short branch of just over a mile in length was another to be originally constructed as a tramroad. Opened in 1827, conversion to a railway on a slightly amended alignment took place in 1867. It left the main line about half a mile to the south of Ruabon station, just before the Llangollen line branched off, then curved north-west to reach Plas Madoc Colliery, already served by the line to Pontcysyllte, crossing that line on the level and finally curving south-west to serve brickworks on the west side of Acrefair. Most of this line closed in 1927, with a short stub from Acrefair to Delph surviving until 1953.

Johnstown & Hafod station, north of Ruabon. (Leslie Oppitz Collection)

5
Lines to Denbigh and Mold

Rhyl to Denbigh
Denbigh to Corwen
Denbigh to Mold
Chester to Mold

Denbigh station. (Lens of Sutton)

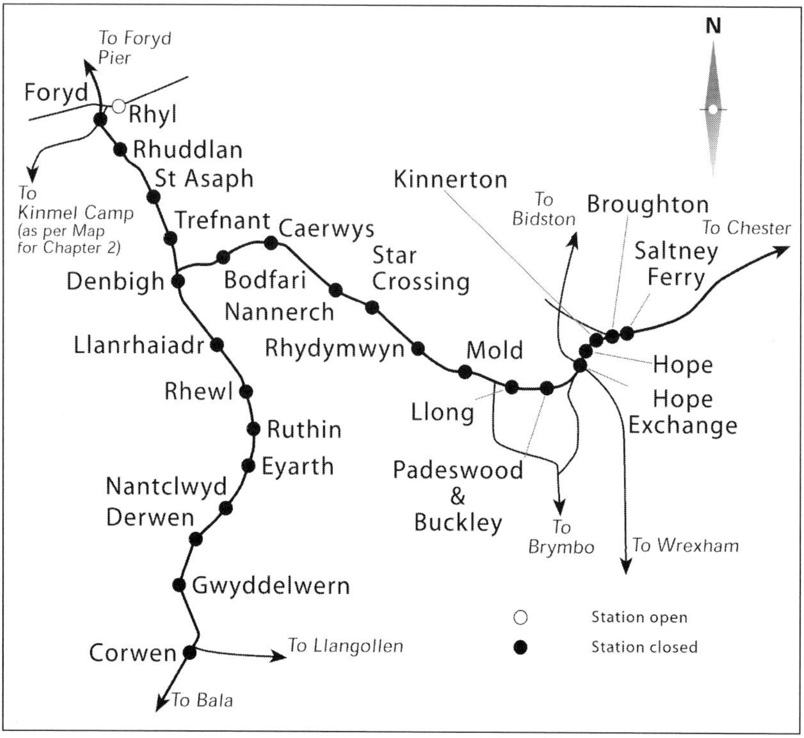

Denbigh, or Denbych, meaning 'Little Fortress', has a long and proud history as a border and fortress town. Fought over by the English and Welsh for hundreds of years, and later serving as a Royalist base during the English Civil War, much survives in ruined form to be explored and enjoyed. There was a castle, town walls, with the eastern section having survived particularly well, and a friary, though modern Denbigh has developed somewhat to the north and east of the original fortified town.

Rhyl to Denbigh

The first railway to reach Denbigh was the Vale of Clwyd line running south from Foryd junction on the Chester & Holyhead

Rhuddlan station, Rhyl to Denbigh line. (Leslie Oppitz Collection)

5th King's Regiment returning to Trefnant, Rhyl to Denbigh line. (Leslie Oppitz Collection)

(Above and below) St Asaph station, Rhyl to Denbigh line. (Leslie Oppitz Collection)

line west of Rhyl. This flat and largely pastoral vale posed few of the challenges faced by railway engineers in other parts of Wales, so after authorisation in 1856 the Vale of Clwyd Company wasted little time, the line being ready to open by October of 1858. Intermediate stations were provided at Rhuddlan, St Asaph and Trefnant. A station at Foryd, close to the junction, also operated for a while but was primarily built as an exchange platform for the short-lived Foryd Pier line (see Chapter 2) and had closed by April 1885. By 1867 the local company had been absorbed by the LNWR and the line settled down to the minor secondary status it would have for the rest of its existence. Running north to south, the Vale of Clwyd was never going to be part of any important through route but early traffic was sufficient to justify a second platform at both St Asaph and Trefnant stations in 1877. Closure took place in September 1955 to regular passenger traffic, with Trefnant station closing its doors two years previously. Excursion trains continued to use the route for some years after, and a little goods traffic survived until final closure in January 1968.

Not a great deal of this line survives, with the trackbed having been built over both at Trefnant, where a small estate of bungalows occupies the station site, and at St Asaph, where time spent enjoying the magnificent cathedral, on a site sacred since the 6th century, is far more worthwhile than trying to locate the meagre remains of the old railway. At Denbigh a goods shed still remains, isolated in the middle of an industrial estate.

Denbigh to Corwen

Another line promoted by a local company, in this case the Denbigh, Ruthin & Corwen Railway (DR&C), this route formed a natural southward extension to the Vale of Clwyd. Original plans were to forge a way through the Clwydian range to Llangollen but the route as built kept closely to the upper valley of the Clwyd to reach Corwen. Whether the intention was to link up with the GWR line at Corwen is not entirely clear as the DR&C held negotiations with both the GWR and the LNWR before opting for the latter. Relations with the GWR at Corwen were not

Llanrhaiadr station, Denbigh to Corwen line. (Leslie Oppitz Collection)

Ruthin station, Denbigh to Corwen line. (Leslie Oppitz Collection)

Nantclwyd station, Denbigh to Corwen line. (Leslie Oppitz Collection)

Eyarth station, Denbigh to Corwen line. (Leslie Oppitz Collection)

good, as shown by the fact that not only separate offices were kept there but also separate refreshment rooms were provided for each company's passengers. As well as a re-siting of Denbigh station to allow southbound traffic, intermediate stations were provided at Llanrhaiadr, Rhewl, Ruthin, Eyarth, Nantclwyd, Derwen and Gwyddelwern. It also formed part of the route of the popular 'Land Cruises' that British Railways operated on weekdays in the 1950s, which made a circular journey, usually starting from Rhyl, travelling via the Vale of Clwyd to Corwen, south-west through Dolgellau to Barmouth, then round the Cambrian coast to Caernarfon and back to Rhyl along the north coast.

This minor railway, unquestionably rural and not part of any useful through route, was an obvious candidate for early closure to local passenger traffic, which took place in February 1953, though the Mold line service was extended to Ruthin until April 1962. A group of railway ramblers visited Derwen station in 1996 and were delighted to find the original stationmaster and his wife still in residence. She was then 92, her husband a mere 86! Derwen station, unlike most of the others on this line, still stands, now looking out over fields full of sheep and frolicking lambs, rather than locomotives and carriages.

A recent view of Derwen station, Denbigh to Corwen line. (Author)

Denbigh to Mold

Undoubtedly the busiest of the routes to reach Denbigh, the Mold line provided access to both Chester, via Hope and Kinnerton, and to Wrexham via Hope junction and Penyffordd, or via Coed Talon. Promoted by the Mold & Denbigh Junction Railway, the line ran for just under 16 miles along the valleys of the rivers Alyn and Wheeler. Original plans were for the line to divide west of Bodfari, with one branch running north-west towards St Asaph and another running south to Denbigh. By the time the line opened, in September 1869, arrangements were simplified to incorporate only a south facing junction (Mold & Denbigh junction) with the Vale of Clwyd line a mile or so north of Denbigh. Although powers were obtained to construct a north to east curve, south-east of Trefnant, this was never constructed. Stations were provided at Bodfari, Caerwys, Nannerch and Rhydymwyn, with a halt added at Star Crossing, the line's summit, in 1914.

Traffic proved busy – for once a branch line's receipts justified the promoter's predictions – and much of the line was doubled. Further traffic came from industrial sites at the Mold end, including a tin plate works a mile or so west of Mold which retained traffic until 1984. All traffic to the west of Rhydymwyn ceased in April 1962.

Mold station circa 1910. (Lens of Sutton)

Bodfari station, circa 1910. Bodfari was the last station before Denbigh on the line from Chester and Mold. (Lens of Sutton)

Bodfari station lies forlorn after closure and track lifting. (Leslie Oppitz Collection)

Nannerch station circa 1910. After closure this station became an attractive residence, but soon after was demolished to make way for road widening. (Lens of Sutton)

Much of the Denbigh to Mold line was obliterated by improvements to the parallel A541 road, though Star Crossing is a delightful survivor with both platforms and a waiting shelter still in place. Nannerch station suffered a particularly painful fate; it was converted into a private dwelling with a lovely garden planted between the platforms, only for it to be compulsory purchased and demolished to allow realignment of the main road soon afterwards.

Chester to Mold

The Mold Railway was one of the earliest ventures into north-east Wales, being authorised by an 1847 Act of Parliament and opening in August 1849. Backed by and operated by the LNWR (in fact, originally the Chester & Holyhead), the Mold Railway was quick to lose its independence.

Running from a junction with the Chester & Holyhead line at Saltney Ferry, on the south bank of the River Dee, the Mold Railway ran first south-west, and then north-west, largely avoiding the hilly area around Buckley, though a short incline of 1 in 43 was required near Kinnerton. Intermediate stations were provided at Broughton (later Broughton Hall, then Broughton & Bretton) and Llong, with further ones added at Padeswood (1851, later renamed Padeswood & Buckley), Hope (1877, later Hope & Penyffordd) and Kinnerton (1891), together with a station named Saltney Ferry at Mold junction. Hope Exchange Platform, with no road access at all, opened in 1866 to coincide with the opening of the WM&CQ line running north to south, when a west to south curve was built between Hope junction and Penyffordd, which allowed through running between Mold and Chester. An east to south spur was also authorised, and earthworks constructed, but no track was ever laid.

Decline started in the 1950s, with the closure of Hope station in 1952 and Padeswood & Buckley four years later. Chester to Mold passenger services (most ran through to Denbigh or Ruthin) ceased to operate in September 1963, though there are records of unadvertised workmen's services from Broughton & Bretton to Chester operating until September 1963. The line continued in use for goods traffic, but by 1970 it was possible to close Mold junction to Hope junction and run the remaining traffic from Mold via the spur to Penyffordd and Wrexham. Traffic continued to reach Mold by this route until 1984. Station buildings survive at Broughton & Bretton (now a veterinary surgery), Hope & Penyffordd (residential) and Llong. At Rhydymwyn (where sufficient time has now elapsed to reveal that a wartime siding served a top secret factory making shells and mustard gas), both platforms remain, as does a beautifully-restored waiting shelter on the former Chester-bound platform.

6
Llangollen to Morfa Mawddach, the GWR Main Line

Llangollen Railway
Llangollen Canal Tramway
Corwen to Bala
Bala to Llanuwchllyn and the Bala Lake Railway
Llanuwchllyn to Morfa Mawddach

Bala Junction station. (Leslie Oppitz Collection)

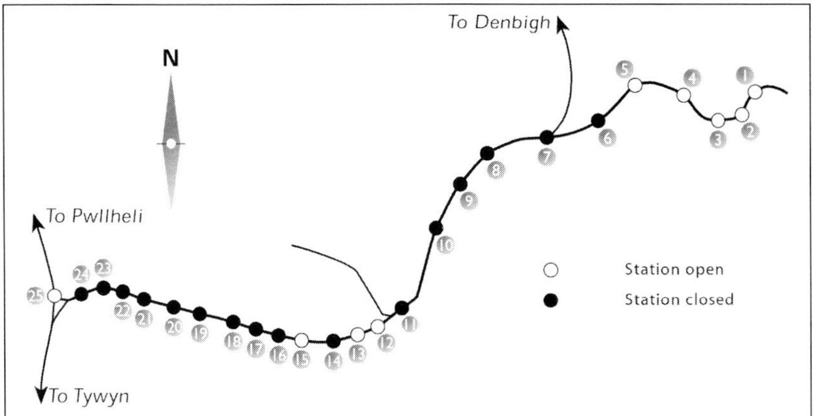

1. Llangollen
2. Berwyn
3. Deeside Halt
4. Glyndyfrdwy
5. Carrog
6. Bonwm Halt
7. Corwen
8. Cynwyd
9. Llandrillo
10. Llandderfel
11. Bala Junction
12. Bala/Bala Lake Halt
13. Llangower Halt
14. Flag Halt
15. Llanuwchllyn
16. Llys Halt
17. Gardeddwen Halt
18. Drws-y-nant
19. Wnion Halt
20. Bont Newydd
21. Dolserau Halt
22. Dolgellau
23. Penmaenpool
24. Arthog
25. Morfa Mawddach (Barmouth Junction)

Llangollen Railway

The line from Llangollen to Corwen opened in 1865, shortly after the Vale of Clwyd line had reached the small town. Forging ever further west, Llandrillo was reached on 16th July 1866, and the remainder to Bala, 12½ miles west of Corwen, opened on 1st April 1868. Shortly afterwards, the next 17¼ miles to Dolgelley (renamed Dolgellau in 1960) opened on 4th August the same year. The line proved sufficiently busy to justify a number of developments and improvements. A passing loop and second platform were installed at Glyndyfrdwy in 1877, and in 1884 Bala Junction station was installed to replace the original Bala station. By the start of the First World War a loop had been installed at Deeside, now the site of Deeside Halt on the preserved section of the line.

Closure was proposed by the Beeching report and, after all through traffic had ceased in 1964, total closure was planned for 18th January 1965. However, damage caused by flooding on 12th and 13th December 1964 brought about a premature closure of the through route, though freight services from Ruabon reached Llangollen until 1968. The track, signalling and much of the infrastructure was removed or demolished quickly after this, although Llangollen, Berwyn and Carrog station buildings survived. Llangollen station then lay derelict for over ten years, an unfortunate eyesore particularly given the station's superb riverside location close to the town centre. However, things were eventually to improve.

The 'new' Llangollen Railway was started in 1975 by a group of enthusiasts who saw the potential for a scenic heritage line through the Dee Valley and were able to secure a lease on Llangollen station. After taking a few years to get established, reopening progressed; Berwyn was reached in 1985, Deeside in 1990, Glyndyfrdwy in 1993 and Carrog in 1996, giving a current total of 7½ miles of track having been re-laid westwards from Llangollen. From Carrog, work is currently ongoing, including the digging out of previously infilled cuttings for a further

Railway ramblers on a 2005 supervised track-walk along the Llangollen Railway leave Berwyn Tunnel. (Author)

Deeside Halt on the Llangollen Railway, with a delightful GWR 'pagoda' waiting shelter installed on the platform. (Author)

Carrog station, east of Corwen. (Author)

Corwen station looking east. (Leslie Oppitz Collection)

An early view, looking west, of Corwen station. (Lens of Sutton)

extension to Corwen, where a new station will be built on open land to the east of the town as the trackbed further west has been sold off and built over with housing. A small halt at Bonwm opened in 1935 on this section and the remains of the platform may still just be discerned. Corwen station site is now the headquaters of the trailer manufacturer Ifor Williams; here it is still possible to see a weighbridge, a goods shed and part of the original platform facing.

Llangollen Canal Tramway

A tramway of 3 ft gauge opened in 1852, from the terminus of the canal feeder at Pentre Felin to serve slate quarries at Moel-y-fan, some 4 miles away above the horseshoe pass. Engineering works included embankments and an incline. Unfortunately, there appear to be no details recorded about its later use or date of closure. Some of this tramway may still be followed as part of a lane or rough trackway.

A recent view of Corwen station building. The platform facing may be seen in the right foreground of the photograph. (Author)

Corwen to Bala

Cynwyd station. All that survives is the remains of the entrance gate to the station approach. (Author)

The first 2 miles of this stretch west of the former site of Corwen station now forms a pleasant footpath and cycleway to the village of Cynwyd, where the station has gone and lorries park where trains once ran, but the remnants of a gently decaying gate to the station entrance may still be seen. At Llandrillo a goods shed remains, hidden by timber in a yard next to a caravan park, while at Llandderfel, all that is left are the remains of wooden steps that used to lead down to the platform from the roadside. Just to the west of here lies a 159-yard long tunnel which is still open and walkable with permission.

At Bala, arrangements changed a number of times over the years. The original station was situated a mile or so south of the town and at the easternmost point of Bala Lake. However, on the opening of the Blaenau Ffestiniog line a station was provided at the junction, ¾ mile to the east, and one on the latter line situated in the town itself. The original Bala station closed in 1892 but a halt known as Bala Lake or Pen-y-bont Halt occupied the same site between 1934 and 1939. This location in turn now forms the northern terminus of the Bala Lake Railway.

Bala to Llanuwchllyn and the Bala Lake Railway

The trackbed of the section of line alongside Llyn Tegid (Bala Lake) between Bala and Llanuwchllyn is these days occupied by the 2 ft gauge Bala Lake Railway. It was along this stretch that 'Flag Halt', later Glanllynn Halt, was situated. Flag Halt was originally private, built for one of the original company's directors, Sir Watkin Williams-Wynn, who had a property on the opposite side of the lake. When a train was required for Sir Watkin or a member of his household, a flag would be raised at the platform; this also summoned a boat from across the water to complete the journey.

The Bala Lake Railway opened as a narrow gauge line in 1972 and therefore can these days be considered as well established, with more than 35 years of running under its belt. Having been built on a former standard gauge formation, with the original bridges and full size station buildings, gives the Bala Lake line a quite different, much more spacious feel than many other narrow gauge railways, which often find themselves squashed onto tiny ledges or into narrow spaces between buildings.

Some changes and adaptations have taken place, with the station buffet at Llanuwchllyn, formerly the waiting room and the seating section, having been moved from its former site at Morfa Mawddach (Barmouth Junction). The canopy supports were originally at the first station in Pwllheli, but were taken down when it was moved to the current site in 1907. These were reconstructed at Aberdovey until the station there was dismantled in 1979, at which time they moved again to Llanuwchllyn. Also still intact at Llanuwchllyn is the ex-GWR signal box with its original lever frame.

The modern Bala station on the lake railway, showing narrow gauge track but a standard gauge-sized bridge. (Bala Lake Railway)

Llanuwchllyn to Morfa Mawddach

Originally this section was run by two separate concerns, with the Great Western Railway operating the line south from Bala and Cambrian Railways running the section east of Morfa Mawddach. Meeting at Dolgellau, Cambrian Railways briefly operated their own station, a few hundred yards to the west of that of the GWR. Stations were situated at Drws-y-nant and Bont Newydd where road widening obliterated the site shortly after closure. The station buildings at Dolgellau (Dolgelley) stood silently for over a decade, becoming increasingly vandalised until the site was cleared in 1977 and a bypass for the small town built along the course of the line. West of Dolgellau the trackbed was converted to a footpath in the 1970s and the line may be followed all the way to the junction with the Cambrian Coast line at Morfa Mawddach, a distance of over 7 miles. Skirting the estuary of the Mawddach, the walk offers fine views of the semi-marine landscape, the slightly more distant mountains, and of the local bird life. Points of railway interest include the former signal box at Penmaenpool, now used as a visitor centre by the RSPB and complete with a signal still apparently guarding the former level crossing, and the foundations of a concrete platform at Arthog. At Penmaenpool the former layout may not be easily understood by the casual visitor; the wooden platforms were on the east side of the level crossing, next to the signal box, whilst a single track threaded its way through the narrow gap between the George Hotel – virtually unchanged from when the line was open – and the estuary.

This signal box at Penmaenpool station is now used only for bird-watching. (Author)

7
From Llanymynych along the Cambrian Main Line to Caersws

South from Llanymynych
Welshpool & Llanfair Light Railway
Moat Lane Junction to Rhayader
Kerry branch and the Kerry Tramway
Van Railway

Newtown station circa 1910. (Lens of Sutton)

South from Llanymynych

The railway reached Welshpool from the north in August 1860, with the opening of the line south from Oswestry, built by the Oswestry & Newtown Railway. Llanymynych was 30 or so miles down this route from Whitchurch, which at one time formed the most direct route from the north-west of England to Aberystwyth and Cardigan Bay until closure required the traveller to go in and out of Shrewsbury. South of Llanymynych there were stations at Four Crosses, Arddleen (reduced to halt status in 1954) and Pool Quay before reaching Buttington Junction where the line from Shrewsbury joined from the east.

Also in 1860 the Llanidloes & Newtown Company's trains had reached Abermule, with the 'missing link' in between opening in June 1861. Nearly all the services reached Llanidloes, a more important and populous place then than it is now. Aberystwyth was however the long term goal, and a route through Caersws,

A 1960s view of Arddleen, north of Welshpool, after its demotion from a station to a halt. (Lens of Sutton)

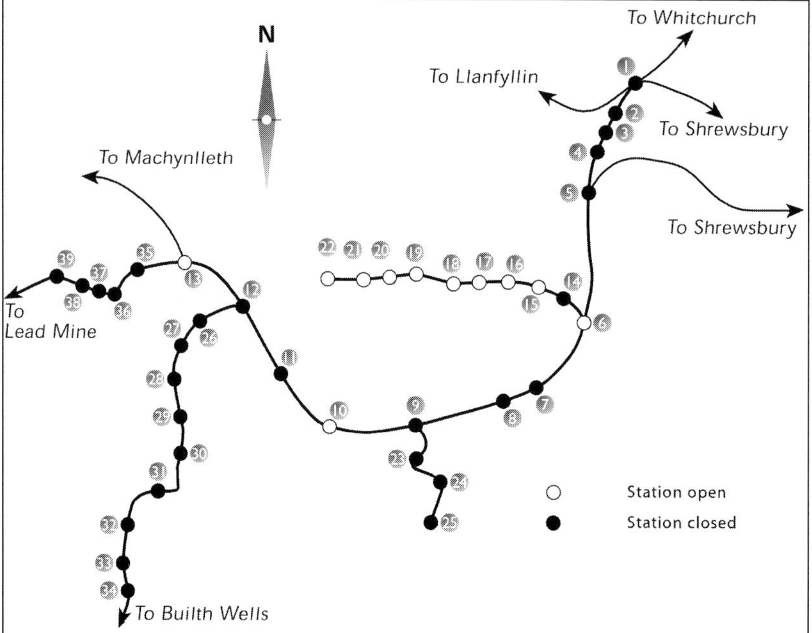

1. Llanymynych
2. Four Crosses
3. Arddleen
4. Pool Quay
5. Buttington
6. Welshpool
7. Forden
8. Montgomery
9. Abermule
10. Newtown
11. Scafell
12. Moat Lane Junction
13. Caersws
14. Seven Stars
15. Raven Square
16. Golfa
17. Sylfaen
18. Castle Caereinion
19. Dolarddyn Crossing
20. Cyfronydd
21. Heniarth
22. Llanfair Caereinion
23. Ffronfraith Halt
24. Goitre Halt
25. Kerry
26. Llandinam
27. Dolwen
28. Llanidloes
29. Tylwch
30. Glan-yr-afon Halt
31. Pant-y-dwr
32. St Harmons
33. Marteg Halt
34. Rhayader
35. Trewythan
36. Red House
37. Trefeglwys
38. Cerist
39. Garth & Van Road

requiring little major engineering, was quickly built and opened in January 1863. An elaborate station at Welshpool was constructed, with others opening with the line at Forden, Montgomery, Abermule, Newtown, Scafell, Moat Lane Junction and Caersws. Improvements gradually took place, with the sections through Welshpool between Buttington Junction and Forden, and Newtown to Moat Lane Junction being doubled. Scafell station closed in 1891 but Scafell Halt, on the same site, was in operation between 1913 and 1955. Abermule was the scene of a tragic head on collision between two trains on the main line in 1921. Fifteen people were killed in an accident caused by the driver of one engine receiving an authorisation tablet for the wrong section of track from a relief signalman.

The inevitable rationalisation commenced in the 1960s, the junction station at Buttington being the first to go, in 1960, followed by Moat Lane Junction on closure of the Llanidloes line in 1962. The double track sections were singled in 1964 and services between Welshpool and Oswestry ceased in January 1965. In June 1965 Forden, Montgomery and Abermule all closed

A contemporary postcard of the 1921 accident at Abermule. (Leslie Oppitz Collection)

Montgomery station after closure. Note that the trackbed has been raised to reduce the risk of flooding from the nearby River Severn. (Leslie Oppitz Collection)

on the same day. Improvements in journey times between Birmingham and the Mid Wales coast did result from these changes, and an irregular service of six trains per day to and from Aberystwyth in 1990 has now increased to eight with departures at regular two-hour intervals.

Mention should be made of the 1992 closure of the fine station at Welshpool. A bypass road to the east of the town was put straight through the line of the railway, which was pushed away from the town, when the addition of two bridges to the bypass could have kept the railway on its original course. The old station at Welshpool became separated from the new alignment, and an anonymous concrete platform with open and exposed approach ramps over the new road was constructed in its place. Fortunately the old station, a listed building, survives, remaining in use for retail purposes, and may therefore still be readily viewed.

Welshpool & Llanfair Light Railway

The Welshpool & Llanfair Light Railway was locally promoted to aid the transport of agricultural produce outwards and supplies of coal and building materials inwards to the Banwy Valley. Proposals for both standard and narrow gauge lines were put forward in the 19th century, but eventually authorisation was granted under a Light Railway Order in 1901 for a line between Welshpool main line station and Llanfair Caereinion. Part of the line though Welshpool was built along the course of an old tramroad, which operated between 1818 and the mid 1850s, linking a quarry near Brook Street with the Montgomery Canal. The line opened to passengers in April 1903, having been constructed at the 'wide narrow gauge' of 2 ft 6 inches. In the centre of Welshpool, the line ran through streets and in gaps between buildings to connect with the standard gauge railway at the main line station. Intermediate stations, mostly merely consisting of small shelters with gravelled areas at rail level serving as 'platforms', were provided at Seven Stars, Raven Square, Golfa, Castle Caereinion, Cyfronydd, Heniarth, and Llanfair Caereinion. In 1904 two further stations were added, at Sylfaen and Dolarddyn, while a passing loop was constructed at Castle Caereinion in 1907.

Without heavy freight traffic such as coal or slate the little railway failed to thrive. Although the 1914–18 war brought a surge of business, it fell away again in the 1920s, and after grouping (1923) the line became the property of the GWR. Passenger services ceased in February 1931 after the Great Western had started to run a bus service along the parallel main road. Again, the onset of war brought an increase in use, but by the 1950s only one train per week was required for the agricultural traffic. The last commercial goods train ran in November 1956, and by then moves were already afoot to try to preserve this unique rural railway. By 1959 negotiations with British Railways were at a stage where volunteers were able to begin clearing overgrowth. They formed the Welshpool & Llanfair Light Railway Preservation Company Limited in 1960 and leased the line from BR at the end of 1962.

Welshpool & Llanfair Light Railway. Raven Square station, where the building from Eardisley in Herefordshire has been re-erected. (Author)

Welshpool & Llanfair Light Railway at Raven Square. All clear for Llanfair! (Author)

With an unusual gauge it was difficult for the railway to obtain locomotives or suitable rolling stock, but it was discovered that the Admiralty operated a 2 ft 6 inch line in Kent and from there in 1961 the W&L was able to acquire a number of surplus carriages and wagons. These were much needed in order to re-establish the passenger service that commenced on 6th April 1963 between Llanfair Caereinion and Castle Caereinion. Unfortunately at this time Welshpool Borough Council decided that they did not want the new company to work trains over the town section, and this part of the line saw its last train in August 1963. The W&L was therefore forced to cut back its operations to the present terminus at Raven Square, where the former station building at Eardisley (Herefordshire) was purchased and reconstructed.

At the time of writing, proposals have been made to extend the track back into the town itself, with Welshpool Town Council announcing that a feasibility study would be carried out into the plans. The W&L does not at this stage appear to be directly involved.

Moat Lane Junction to Rhayader

The Llanidloes & Newtown Railway received Royal Assent in August 1853 and opened, after many financial ups and downs, in August 1859. South of Llanidloes two companies were involved, the Llanidloes & Newtown and the Manchester & Milford Railway. The latter had grandiose plans to forge westwards, going from Llangurig to Devil's Bridge and thence via Pencader to Carmarthen and Milford Haven, with a branch to Aberystwyth, roughly along what was to become the route of the Vale of Rheidol line. Unfortunately the M&M only managed to build a section of just over 3 miles, from Penpontbren junction, a couple of miles south of Llanidloes, to Llangurig. It was completed by February 1864, by which time ambitions further west had been abandoned, and it is recorded that only one goods train ever reached Llangurig. Meanwhile the Mid Wales Railway from Llanidloes south to Rhayader, Builth Wells and beyond opened in September 1864.

Between Moat Lane Junction and Llanidloes, stations were provided at Llandinam and Dolwen, whilst south of Llanidloes there were stations at Tylwch, Pantydwr and St Harmons. Halts were added in GWR days after grouping at Glan-yr-afon (1928) and Marteg (1931).

Serving a largely static and very rural population, with no major mining or quarrying enterprises providing traffic, the line settled to a quiet and unremarkable existence. As such it was a prime candidate for closure, which after vigorous local protests took place in December 1962 to both passengers and through goods traffic. Traffic supplying cement to a new reservoir construction at Llanidloes kept the northern section open until October 1967.

Several station buildings have survived along this route, and although much of the formation is intact a number of river crossings are now in poor condition and exploration of this line

Rock cutting near Tylwch, south of Llanidloes. (Author)

Goods shed at Rhayader. (Author)

may perhaps be easier if points of interest are visited by car. The fine station building at Llanidloes remains in use as offices, though in 1990 a new bypass was built on and at a lower level than the railway formation, leaving the building's original purpose quite difficult to recognise. Llandinam, Dolwen and Tylwch stations are in private occupation, but the site at St Harmons was quickly built over by new housing. A fine sheer rock cutting may also still be seen just south of Tylwch. At Rhayader, with its huge livestock market space almost overshadowing the picturesque little town, the station building, platform and goods shed can still be viewed in the compound of a council depot.

Kerry branch and the Kerry Tramway

As soon as the Llanidloes & Newtown Railway had reached the region, a proposal for a line to serve the area south of the main

A 1960s' view of Abermule station, with the bay platform, previously used by Kerry branch trains, still in good condition. (Lens of Sutton)

line was made by Mr John Wilkes Poundley, known also for his development of the Kerry breed of sheep. A steeply graded line up the valley of the River Mule from Abermule was swiftly built and opened in March 1863. The Kerry branch served only farmsteads and other isolated communities, but did its job well for many years though never providing more than a minimal service. Closure to passengers was in February 1931 and all use ended in May 1956.

The Kerry branch started from its own platform at Abermule, adjoining that serving the coast-bound main line. On a gradient of about 1 in 43, with the tightest of curves, trains were restricted to a maximum speed of no more than 9 miles per hour. Tiny intermediate halts were provided at Ffronfraith and Goitre, and there was quite a substantial station at Kerry, where a resident stationmaster ruled the roost in passenger days.

Though now almost all in private hands, much of the formation can still be followed, albeit with the necessary permission. All traces of the platform used by Kerry trains at Abermule station

Ffronfraith on the Kerry branch. This tiny halt was built straight despite the obvious curvature of the line at this point. (Author)

Kerry station today. (Author)

have been removed, but the tiny platform at Ffronfraith, built straight despite the curvature of the line here, remains. The site of Goitre Halt has been obliterated but Kerry station is a delightful and remarkable relic, with the station building (now residential), platform and an engine shed still standing in the environs of a farm. Just east of Kerry station a 2 ft gauge, steam operated line, some 5 miles in total length, reached further into the wilds to serve agricultural and forestry locations. Known as the Kerry Tramway, it saw intermittent use from its opening in 1888 until around 1922. The Kerry Tramway was at its busiest around 1917 when a small prisoner of war camp was in operation near Lower Rhos. Earthworks were generally minimal but can be traced in places, as can the sites of some of the bridges. The best surviving relic is, however, a former locomotive shed about ¾ mile south of Kerry, now used only as a shelter for cattle.

Van Railway

The hills to the west of Caersws and to the north of Llanidloes proved to be an abundant source of lead, and by the 1850s no fewer than sixteen companies were vying to develop mines to exploit the source of this metal. Eventually a consortium that became known as the Van Mining Company Ltd took charge, and by the 1860s required a railway to transport their valuable commodity to the cities, where, as sanitation and drainage was developing, there was a desperate need for lead for piping. Although Llanidloes was only a mile or two away, major engineering would have been required and instead a line of just under 7 miles in length was built to Caersws, following the 'U' shaped valleys of the Rivers Carno, Cerist and Trannon. Original opening for freight took place in August 1871, though the line appears to have been in some use on an unofficial basis for a while before that. The need for a service to get workmen and other staff up to the mines prompted opening of a passenger service, which commenced in 1873. Starting from a separate station at Caersws, platforms were provided for passengers at Trewythen, Red House, Trefeglwys (later Pwll-glas), Cerist and

Garth & Van Road. In an area with only isolated farmsteads and a few rows of terraced cottages, nothing even worthy of being termed a village, support for a passenger service was minimal and it proved to be one of the most short-lived of such routes anywhere in Britain, closing in 1879 (no precise record of the date appears to exist). Meanwhile the lead mines remained busy and profitable for a further ten years, and Cambrian Railways also found the crushed stone produced as a by-product of lead extraction to be excellent ballast, being impervious to weed growth. However, the mines closed in 1893 and accordingly so did the railway. Revival came in 1896, as the Cambrian wanted more ballast, and some smaller scale mining resumed until about 1920. After that time fewer and fewer trains ran, and final closure took place in November 1940.

Parts of the lead mines and their associated buildings and inclines may still be explored today, as can the head of the line leading eastwards. At Garth & Van Road, the quarrymen's cottages have slate coverings on their western elevation as well as their roof – such is the exposed position they were built on. A

Van Railway; this tunnel led to lead mine workings at Van. (Author)

Caersws station (Van Railway). (Author)

Caersws station. No money or tickets have been passed under this hatch since 1879! (Author)

number of mileposts survive along the route, as does a former weighbridge cabin at Pwll-glas, now incorporated as a feature in a private garden. Much of the trackbed can still be followed as a low embankment alongside the banks of the tiny rivers. At Caersws remarkably little has changed. The engine shed, now a listed building, remains in use for light engineering purposes, and the station building with platform is an even more remarkable survivor. Inside the station is a ticket office, with a little hatch under which tickets and money were exchanged, virtually untouched since last used in 1879.

8
Beyond Caersws to Aberystwyth

Caersws to Aberystwyth
Mawddwy Railway
Corris Railway
Funicular railway at the Centre for Alternative Technology
Aberystwyth to Devil's Bridge (Vale of Rheidol Light Railway)
Aberystwyth Constitution Hill Cliff Railway
Plynlimon & Hafan Tramway

Just a nameboard! Surely the most minimalist station in Wales; at Llanbadarn on the Vale of Rheidol line. (Author)

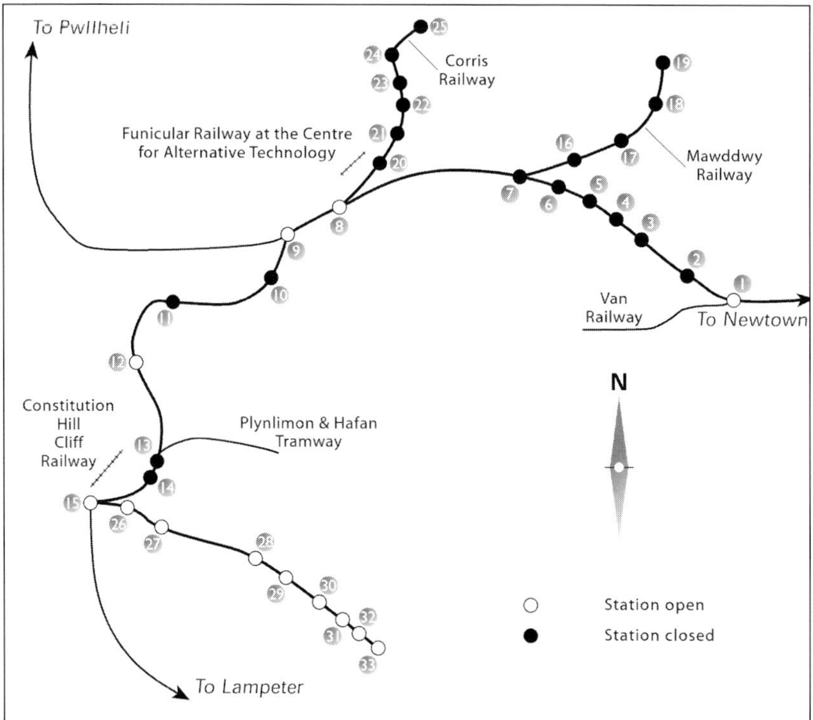

1. Caersws
2. Pontdolgoch
3. Carno
4. Talerddig
5. Llanbrynmair
6. Commins Coch Halt
7. Cemmes Road
8. Machynlleth
9. Dovey Junction
10. Glandyfi
11. Ynyslas
12. Borth
13. Llandre
14. Bow Street
15. Aberystwyth
16. Cemmaes
17. Aberangell
18. Mallwyd
19. Dinas Mawddwy
20. Ffidd Gate
21. Llwyngwern
22. Esgairgeiliog
23. Corris
24. Garneddwen
25. Aberllefenni
26. Llanbadarn
27. Glanrafon
28. Capel Bangor
29. Nantyronen
30. Aberffrwd
31. Rheidol Falls
32. Rhiwfron
33. Devil's Bridge

Caersws to Aberystwyth

This section was the first to be completed by the Aberystwyth Company, partly to connect to the Newtown and Machynlleth line to the east and partly simply because it was the easiest to construct. Aberystwyth prospered and its combination of university (the oldest in Wales), library centre and tourist destination keeps it busy to this day. The library is very much the premier repository for books in the Welsh language, housing around five million volumes including the 12th century *Black Book of Carmarthen*, the oldest surviving text known in the language.

There is a little known connection between the railway and the wonderfully gothic original main building of the university. In order to publicise the growing resort, Cambrian Railways came up with the idea of offering a free week's board and lodging in a palatial hotel to anyone who bought a return ticket from London. The promoter believed that this offer would pack the town with visitors, and accordingly spent £80,000 on what was one of the most spectacular hotels built anywhere in Britain. But the hotel

Machynlleth station in Cambrian days. (Leslie Oppitz Collection)

A 1970s' view of Aberystwyth station. (Leslie Oppitz Collection)

did not pay its way and by 1870 it was closed and derelict. The building was then bought by the university for a mere £10,000, restored and converted to academic use.

Reaching Aberystwyth in the summer of 1864, including intermediate stations at Pontdolgoch, Carno, Llanbrynmair, Cemmes Road, Machynlleth, Ynyslas, Borth, Llanfihangel (later Llandre) and Bow Street, the line quickly became taken over by Cambrian Railways. Talerddig station opened in 1910 and a halt was provided at Commins Coch in 1931.

Sufficient land was purchased to allow for future doubling of the line, but this was never required. A short-lived minor branch led to a ferry across the River Dovey near Ynyslas between 1863 and 1867. Improvements were gradually made, reflecting the increased level of use. Lengthening of the platform at Dovey Junction (originally Glandovey Junction) was carried out in 1890; sidings to accommodate the extensive army camps around

Aberystwyth before and around the start of the First World War and passing loops with second platforms were installed at Llandre and Borth stations in 1911.

At grouping in 1923 the line became part of the GWR, and a direct service, known as the 'Cambrian Coast Express', with a restaurant car, from Paddington to Aberystwyth was instituted. New buildings were constructed at Aberstwyth station and the approach to the station doubled. The 'Cambrian Coast Express' ran until 1967, by which time significant rationalisation to the line had commenced. Intermediate stations at Bow Street, Llandre, Ynyslas and Glandyfi had closed in 1965 leaving only Borth between Aberystwyth and Dovey Junction. Changes also took place at Aberystwyth station, with the layout drastically reduced, retaining only a single platform and loop for main line services. At the southern end of the station the platform formerly used by Carmarthen line services was taken over by the Vale of Rheidol Railway and part of the terminus building is now a public house with tables and chairs filling the covered courtyard area directly behind the buffer stops.

Aberystwyth station today. Note the change of layout with ground level platforms now provided for the Vale of Rheidol trains. (Author)

Mawddwy Railway

Many railways were built to take tradable material away from the places they were supposed to serve; but the Mawddwy was built on the premise that there would also be tourist traffic up the line. Opened in October 1867, a line of 6½ miles left the main line east of Cemmes Road station. Originally there was just one intermediate station, at Cemmaes (Cemmes until 1911), but later two further stations opened, at Aberangell (1873) and Mallwyd (1896).

Traffic proved disappointing. The line served too small a population for a viable passenger service; though two tramways were built to bring slate down from nearby quarries this was never on the scale of the larger enterprises to the north, and although undoubtedly a delightful location for fishing, Dinas Mawddwy never became a mainstream tourist destination. Passenger traffic ceased in 1901 and complete closure followed in 1908, the poor condition of some of the timber bridges along the route hastening its demise.

Cemmaes (previously Cemmes) station, Mawddwy Railway in the 1920s. (Leslie Oppitz Collection)

However, it appears that the line was sorely missed by the local community, and, after pressure from local dignitaries and councillors, was taken over by Cambrian Railways and reopened in July 1911. The early years of the revival proved to be the Mawddwy's heyday; timber, required in great quantities for the war effort, was transported down the line from the great expanse of forest at the head of the Dovey Valley.

After grouping, the line, as with the entire Cambrian system, became the property of the GWR, who soon became aware of the lack of revenue being generated. Final closure to passengers took place in January 1931 whilst slate and general freight traffic enabled the line to hang on until July 1951, though the last train had run on 5th September 1950.

Close to the terminus station at Dinas Mawddwy a short tramway with a steep incline served the Minllyn Slate Quarry on the hillside to the west of the station. At Aberangell, a more substantial set of tramways, known as the Hendre Ddu system,

At Aberangell on the Mawddwy Railway, this code on the brickwork indicates that the remains of a bridge are still the responsibility of the British Railways Property Board, some 65 years after closure! (Author)

Dinas Mawddwy station today. (Author)

served further quarries and also saw use for the timber traffic; these lines were closed and lifted by the early 1940s.

At Dinas Mawddwy, the station site was taken over after closure by Meirion Mill Ltd who have prospered both as manufacturers of high quality woollen garments and also as a tourist/shopping destination in an area not flush with other attractions. In 1975 it appeared that they were even looking to start a revival of the railway, as a 2 ft gauge line was laid along the old formation for six hundred yards to serve a picnic area. However, this railway did not prove viable and was closed and lifted in 1977. The station building, which along with its platform can be clearly seen on the right as you enter Meirion Mill, was for many years used as a shop by the company, but in 2005 was sold off and converted to a private dwelling. The former engine shed is still, however, in use for retail purposes.

The old trackbed may be followed, with permission, to Aberangell, and much of the former Hendre Ddu system can still be traced by those who know where to look for it. At Aberangell, the abutments of a substantial bridge over the Angell may still be viewed. A yellow painted box on the brickwork with a three letter code indicates that these remains still belong to the British Railways Property Board; over 65 years after the last train crossed the bridge. The southernmost section down to Cemmes Road is largely in private hands but parts of the formation can still be viewed as a slight embankment running through field pastures.

Twelve years after it had opened in 1867, the *Gossiping Guide to Wales* wrote: 'Now if you were to search Great Britain over, and had to say where would be the most unlikely place to see a railway station, you would say "At Dinas Mawddwy." And yet there you would find one.'

Corris Railway

The 2 ft 3 inch gauge Corris Railway was authorised by an Act of Parliament in 1864 but in reality had started in April 1859 when a horse-worked tramway known as the Corris, Machynlleth & River Dovey Tramroad began to transport slate to Derwenlas on the estuary of the Afon Dyfi. The section from Machynlleth to Derwenlas proved to be very short-lived, being replaced by exchange sidings as soon as the standard gauge line reached Machynlleth.

Passenger traffic was authorised in 1878 after a change of ownership, but again official approval was rather belated as a passenger service had been running since the early 1870s using open wagons to convey quarry workers and visitors. At first, passenger services ran only from Machynlleth to Corris, but the route was extended to the line's northern terminus at Aberllefenni in 1887. Stations were originally provided only at Machynlleth and Corris, both of which had delightful little overall roofs, but later further halts were added at Ffridd Gate (1887), Llwyngwern (1884), Esgairgeiliog (1884), Garneddwen (1887) and Aberllefenni (1887).

The line continued to run efficiently and quite profitably for many years, reaching no fewer than 150,000 passenger journeys per year by 1900, but closures of the quarries started in 1906 and from that time onwards it never again showed a profit. As well as slate and passengers, the line hauled timber extracted from the Dyfi Forest in the period from the First World War to the 1930s. There was also a steady stream of traffic in coal and general goods to the quarries and communities served by the railway. However, shortly after purchasing the Corris in 1930, the GWR chose to close the line to passengers, services ceasing in January 1931.The line ceased to operate after it was breached by floods in August 1948 and repair was not considered viable. Track lifting took place in 1950.

Closure at this time proved fortunate in one respect, in that the Talyllyn Railway (see Chapter 9), which shares the 2 ft 3 inch gauge, was being revived as a preserved line and was able to purchase and therefore preserve the locomotives that had until that time been working the Corris. Proposals for restoring the Corris Railway, or at least part of it, were developed in the 1970s but it is only in comparatively recent years that a section between Corris and Maespoeth has been reopened. The long term aim is to rebuild 2½ miles of the old line, from Corris to Tan-y-coed, about midway between the original stations at Esgairgeiliog and Llwyngwern.

A visit to the Corris today can combine travelling on the restored section with some time spent exploring one or more of the several horse drawn or gravity powered tramways which brought slate down to the railway. Most of these are now adopted as public footpaths; the best are perhaps the Aberllefenni Quarry tramway and the Ratgoed Tramway north of Aberllefenni, which served Cymerau Quarry and Ratgoed Quarry.

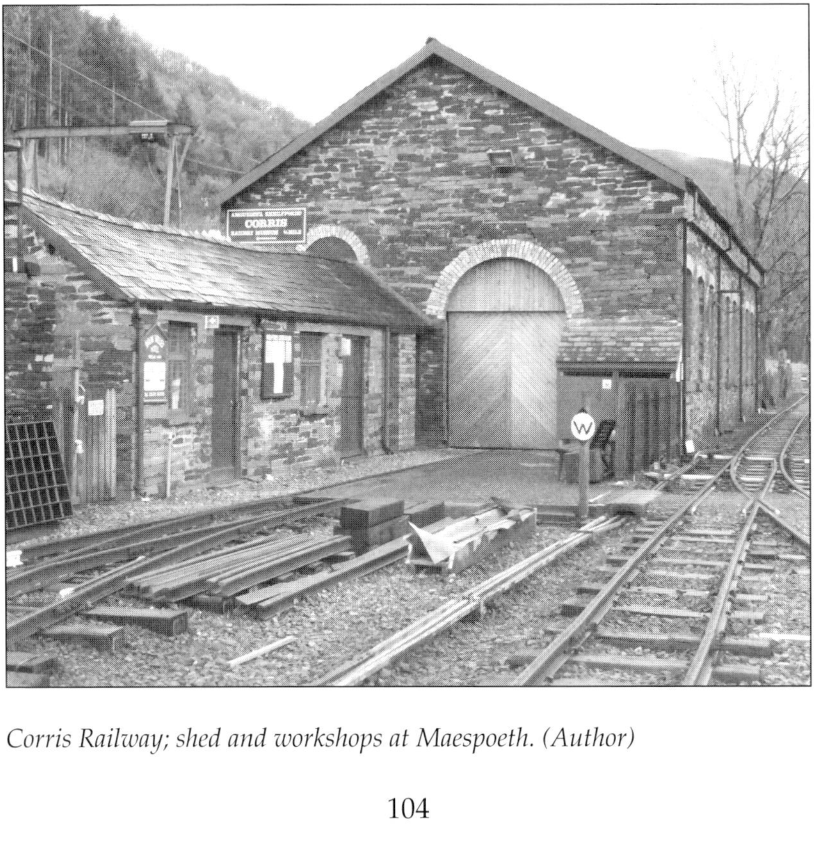

Corris Railway; shed and workshops at Maespoeth. (Author)

Funicular railway at the Centre for Alternative Technology

If you take the A487 road north out of Machynlleth, you will see signs directing you to what is known as the 'Centre for Alternative Technology'. Occupying the site of a former slate quarry, the aim was originally to form a community dedicated to eco-friendly principles and to try out alternative technologies and sources of energy and power; later it became a somewhat unusual tourist destination. One of the developments was a water-powered funicular railway to take visitors up and down the steep slope of the former quarry side. Opened in May 1992, the funicular was built with double track to the unusual gauge of 5 ft 6 inches to allow greater stability. Steeper than most such lines with a gradient of 34 degrees, the line is 58 yards in length and

Funicular railway at the Centre for Alternative Technology near Machynlleth. (Author)

gains 98 ft of height. Power comes from water entering the tank of the upper vehicle, which, linked by cable to its twin, travels down the incline and forces the other carriage upwards. Multiple braking systems are in operation to ensure safety.

It is hoped that joint tickets will be available for both this unusual line and the Corris, once the latter has completed its extension to what will be within comfortable walking distance of the technology centre.

Aberystwyth to Devil's Bridge (Vale of Rheidol Light Railway)

The 1 ft 11 ¾ inch gauge Vale of Rheidol Railway, opened on 22nd December 1902 and nowadays well established as one of the 'Great Little Trains of Wales', has a story somewhat different to that of its narrow gauge neighbours to the north. It never closed; the decline in freight traffic being gradually offset by a growing tourist trade. For many years the Vale of Rheidol had the distinction of being both the last steam railway and the last narrow gauge passenger railway to be owned by British Rail.

Since 1968 the Vale of Rheidol has used the former Carmarthen route platforms at the main station in Aberystwyth, but prior to this, it had its own station just to the south, past which a short branch ran to the harbour until 1924.

Stations were provided at Aberystwyth, Llanbadarn, Capel Bangor, Nantyronen and Devil's Bridge. Further stations were opened at Glanrafon, Aberffrwd, Rheidol Falls and Rhiwfron within two years of the line's opening. At the height of the line's prosperity, in 1912, consideration was given to converting the line to electric traction, using hydro-electric power from the River Rheidol. The First World War saw closure of the Rheidol Lead Mine and a gradual reduction in use of the line, eventually leading to withdrawal of year-round passenger services in 1930, and complete closure during the Second World War. Ownership of the line passed to British Railways in 1948, and though freight traffic ceased in 1964, it survived right through the whole era of

Devil's Bridge, terminus of the Vale of Rheidol Light Railway. (Author)

nationalisation until 1989, when ownership passed to a charitable trust.

Devil's Bridge is famous for its waterfalls and three bridges, these making quite a spectacular sight being built one on top of the other. According to legend, the lowest bridge was built by the Devil himself to let a local woman rescue her cow which had somehow got to the other side of the gorge. Expecting the woman to walk across to get it, his one condition was that he received the soul of the first living creature to cross the bridge. However, he was tricked by the lady who got her pet dog to run across first – thus leaving the Devil with a soul of a dog!

The Aberystwyth Constitution Hill Cliff Railway

The Aberystwyth Cliff Railway opened in 1896 and operated on a water balance system until electrification in 1921. A pair of powerful motor and high-tensile steel cables, supported by a sophisticated electronic safety system, hauls the carriages to the summit at a stately 4 miles per hour. The railway is approx 210 yards long and rises to a height of 328 ft above sea level.

In the mid-section of the journey the railway is in a deep cutting where 12,000 tons of rock was excavated during construction to allow the winding footpath to cross overhead on a series of bridges. The unique design of the undulating track and tilted carriages are the work of George Croydon Marks, a man who played a key role in several projects during the golden age of funicular construction and later made his name in politics as Lord Marks, the liberal peer, and also in the retail trade after forming a partnership with a certain Mr Spencer.

Plynlimon & Hafan Tramway

The Plynlimon & Hafan Tramway was a 2 ft 3inch gauge line which ran eastwards from Llanfihangel (later known as Llandre) station on Cambrian Railways via the village of Talybont and the Afon Leri Valley towards Plynlimon Fawr, to serve the lead mines at Bwlch Glas and stone quarries around Hafan. The line was a little over 7 miles long and despite running a short-lived passenger service, it served no communities of more than 100 people. From early 1897 freight services began on the line, but on 5th June that year an accident occurred close to the level crossing at Glanfred where a train was derailed by a piece of timber lying across the track, leading to the death of one of the train staff. Formal opening to passengers took place on 28th March 1898, although trains only ran on Mondays, connecting with Cambrian Railways' Market Day Special to Aberystwyth. The majority of passenger trains stopped at Talybont as there were few houses to be served further east of that village.

The passenger service only ran until the summer of 1899 and the entire company went into voluntary liquidation in December 1899, the last train having run some time before. The track remained in place until 1914 when it was taken up, though a stretch of line through Bwlchglas Farm apparently remained

Plynlimon & Hafan Tramway. Intact formation over 100 years after closure. (Author)

intact until scrapped by the farmer in 1926. Though the Plynlimon & Hafan was built to the same 2 ft 3 inch gauge as the Corris and Talyllyn Railways the P&H's loading gauge was slightly taller and wider than its two northern neighbours, which meant that neither line was interested in buying any of the P&H rolling stock after it closed.

Today the trackbed formation from Pontbrengeifr to the Hafan incline is largely open and can be walked; much of the formation of the mineral extensions at the top of the incline is also traceable. Between Pontbrengeifr and Talybont sections of the formation run through open but private pastureland and remain intact, but others have been eroded away by the Afon Leri and are heavily overgrown in places. There is now nothing to see of the former exchange sidings at Llandre, where a substantial new residence has been built on the former station site.

9
The West Coast and the Lleyn Peninsula

Dovey Junction to Morfa Mawddach
Fairbourne Railway
Talyllyn Railway
Morfa Mawddach to Pwllheli
Nantlle Railway
Afon Wen to Caernarfon

Afon Wen to Caernarfon line; at the site of Chwilog station, children play where trains once ran. (Author)

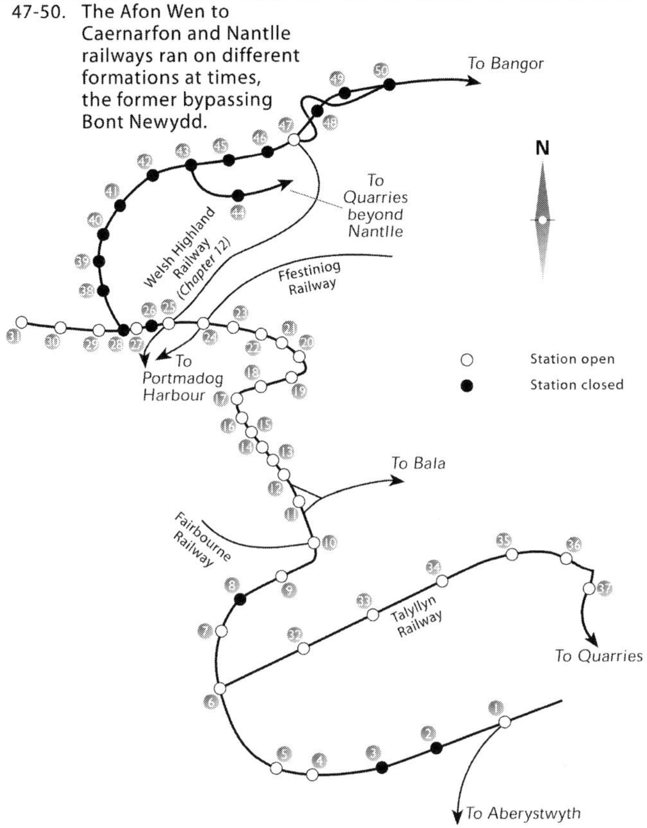

1. Dovey Junction
2. Gogarth Halt
3. Abertafol Halt
4. Penhelig
5. Aberdovey
6. Tywyn
7. Tonfanau
8. Llangelynin Halt
9. Llwyngwril
10. Fairbourne
11. Morfa Mawddach or Barmouth Junction
12. Barmouth
13. Llanaber Halt
14. Talybont Halt
15. Dyffryn Ardudwy
16. Llanbedr
17. Pensarn
18. Llandanwg Halt
19. Harlech
20. Tygwyn Halt
21. Talsarnau
22. Llandecwyn Halt
23. Penrhyndeudraeth
24. Minffordd
25. Porthmadog
26. Black Rock Halt
27. Criccieth
28. Afon Wen
29. Penychain
30. Abererch
31. Pwllheli
32. Pendre
33. Rhydyronen
34. Brynglas
35. Dolgoch
36. Abergynolwyn
37. Nant Gwernol
38. Chwilog
39. Llangybi
40. Ynys
41. Brynkir
42. Pant Glas
43. Penygroes
44. Nantlle
45. Groeslon
46. Llanwnda
47. Dinas Junction
48. Bont Newydd
49. Pant
50. Caernarfon

Dovey Junction to Morfa Mawddach

The Aberystwyth & Welch (*sic*) Coast Railway originally intended to take their line straight along the coast, crossing the River Dovey between Ynyslas and Aberdovey, with a short connecting line to Machynlleth along the south side of the river. Initially a ferry service was provided across the Dovey in anticipation of the viaduct, but by the 1860s when Cambrian Railways had taken over the Aberystwyth Company, plans were being reconsidered. The first section to be constructed north of the Dovey was a fairly straightforward 11 or so miles across the flood meadows between Aberdovey Harbour (for many years the point of outward transport for the local slate) and Llwyngwril, and this isolated line opened to traffic in November 1863. By 1865 a further 3¾ miles to what became Barmouth Junction and a 5 mile section inland to Penmaenpool was also ready.

The River Dovey crossing was eventually abandoned in favour of a route along the northern bank of the river. This was in itself

Aberdovey station in Cambrian Railways days; one of the canopies was later moved to Llanuwchllyn on the Bala Lake Railway. (Leslie Oppitz Collection)

a challenging stretch to construct, with tunnels required at Frongoch and Morfor. Even more complex was the route through Aberdovey; with the line forced away from the harbour it required two further tunnels and heavy earthworks to forge a way through on the landward side. Once this section was opened, in 1867, the station at Aberdovey Harbour closed and a new one was provided at the west end of the town. This coincided with completion of the route to Pwllheli, which in turn linked with the route from Afon Wen to Caernarfon that had opened at the same time.

Stations were provided on opening at Glandovey Junction (later Dovey Junction), Aberdovey (replacing the temporary station at the harbour), Towyn (Tywyn) where exchange sidings with the Talyllyn Railway were constructed, Llwyngwril, Barmouth Ferry (later Fairbourne) and Barmouth Junction (now Morfa Mawddach). A station at Tonfanau was constructed in 1896 though this was initially private and only appeared in the public timetable after 1903. An army base here in the early 20th century at one time generated significant traffic. Halts were also constructed at Gogarth (1923), Abertafol (1935), Penhelig (1933) and Llangelynin (1930). In April 2008 the trackbed and platform at Dovey Junction was rebuilt at a higher level to aid protection against flooding. Gogarth and Abertafol Halts, situated in isolated spots on the north bank of the Dovey, both closed in 1985.

On 25th October 1991 Llangelynin became the last place in Wales to lose its railway station, as new health and safety regulations required lighting to the platform and access path that British Rail was not prepared to provide. However, Llangelynin was surely one of the

Llangelynin Halt; the last station to close anywhere in Wales. (Author)

most unlikely places to have ever got a halt in the first place. Consisting of no more than half a dozen cottages arranged somewhat randomly around a narrow track, leading from the main A493 road to the coast, there are no other dwellings within sight. The only other building is the delightful Llangelynin Old Church, a classic example of the typically spartan and somewhat austere Welsh chapel. As it is left unlocked (a rarity in itself these days) a visitor may enter at any time for prayer or just a moment or two of silent contemplation. Tonfanau, Penhelig, Llwyngwril and Morfa Mawddach are lightly used halts and nowadays are request stops only.

Fairbourne Railway

The Fairbourne Railway always strikes the visitor as being something halfway between a typically Welsh narrow gauge line and one of those miniature seaside railways that you used to see running round a circular track behind the promenade. Indeed a potted history of the Fairbourne is included in the most authoritative book on such miniature railways, written by D.J. Croft for the Oakwood Press, which also includes details of the tiny lines that used to exist at Pwllheli and many of the resorts on the north coast.

The Fairbourne Railway opened in 1895, running north for about 1½ miles from Fairbourne village to Penrhyn Point, with the aim of attracting tourists to the coastal area south of the estuary of the Afon Mawddach and also to take passengers between Fairbourne and the ferry across to Barmouth. Although originally constructed at a 2 ft gauge, the line was converted to a 15 inch gauge railway in 1916 and was further reduced to 12¼ inches in 1986. At one time owned by the Barmouth Ferry Company, the line struggled to stay solvent in the 1930s and closed in September 1940.

After a change of ownership the line reopened in 1947 and a number of new steam and diesel locomotives were acquired. The Fairbourne was at its busiest during the era of popular British seaside holidays in the 1950s but suffered a steady decline

Fairbourne Railway; the impressive terminus station. (Author)

Fairbourne Railway; a tiny locomotive is steamed and turned before starting the day's work. (Author)

thereafter. After the second change of gauge in 1986 all the old locomotives were sold off and half sized replicas of narrow gauge engines were acquired, some from a similar line in Brittany. In 1995 the railway was bought by the current owners, the Atkinson and Melton families, who have invested significantly in the railway to keep the locomotives, station infrastructure and rolling stock in their current excellent state of repair.

Talyllyn Railway

To visit or read about the history of the Talyllyn Railway is not only to study the little railway but to become involved in the whole history of railway preservation. Before doing so it first needs to be said that the name 'Talyllyn' remains something of a mystery; a beautiful lake of that name exists a few miles to the east of the railway, but there were apparently never any plans (nor mineral resources to extract) to extend the line to that point.

The Talyllyn Railway was built primarily to serve one slate quarry, at Bryn Eglwys. All but invisible from the main valley

Talyllyn Railway; station and yard at Pendre. (Leslie Oppitz Collection)

Talyllyn Railway; Abergynolwyn station has a lengthy platform which two trains can use at the same time. (Author)

road, and from the present-day terminus of the Talyllyn Railway at Nant Gwernol, this huge quarry once employed 300 men and in its time produced 300,000 tons of slate and slabs. Initially the plan was to build a railway from Bryn Eglwys to Aberdyfi; however, the construction of what became the Cambrian Coast line meant that only the section as far as Towyn (as it was then known) was required. Powers to construct a railway from Tywyn to Abergynolwyn were obtained in 1865 when Parliament passed the Talyllyn Railway Act. Beyond what is now Nant Gwernol station, the line continued into the hills by a series of rope-worked inclines on which the loaded wagons coming down the hill pulled the empty wagons back up. At Nant Gwernol the line is 270 ft above sea level; the quarries are over 400 ft higher. Beyond the first (Alltwyllt) incline was the ½ mile long Galltymoelfre tramway, then the Cantrybedd incline lifted the tracks further to the lowest level of the quarry and eventually, via Beudynewydd incline and a further horse-worked tramway, the line reached the main quarry buildings.

A passenger service was started in November 1866, after being first turned down by the inspector due to the narrow clearances of carriages below some of the bridges. This was overcome by fastening the doors and barring the windows on the side away from the platform, and slewing the track under the bridges; to this day the carriages on the Talyllyn all have doors only on the 'north-west' side.

Bryn Eglwys Quarry finally closed following a serious collapse on Boxing Day 1946, the inevitable result of years of 'pillaring'. After the remaining slate had been brought down, the quarry lay abandoned for several years before the equipment was scrapped. By this time the passenger service had been reduced to a summer-

Talyllyn Railway; rusty rails still climb up and over the Alltwyllt incline. (Author)

only service of two trains each way three times a week. The Talyllyn somehow managed to escape nationalisation in 1948, as officialdom thought it too run-down, and the level of traffic too low, to be worth taking over, and although it was kept going somehow through the summer of 1950, by October of that year it appeared that the railway had closed for good.

But fortunately it was not to be. A group of enthusiasts, led by the noted author and erstwhile canal enthusiast L.T.C. Rolt, called a public meeting in Birmingham and the Talyllyn Railway Preservation Society was formed. Lady Barbara, widow of the former owner Sir Haydn Jones, graciously agreed to let the Society operate the railway for a trial period of three years, after which if the experiment was successful the arrangement would become permanent. The first passenger trains under Preservation Society auspices ran in May 1951, the trial proved successful and the era of railway preservation had begun.

It had always been hoped to open up the former mineral extension for passenger trains and after additional land was purchased, construction began in October 1970. Abergynolwyn station became a passing place, but had to be designed with one long platform accessible in two halves as the carriages only had doors on the one side. Due to a lack of space, the final curve into Nant Gwernol station was built to a tiny 270 ft radius before opening of the extension took place in May 1976.

In recent years efforts have been made to open up the land above Nant Gwernol to walkers and those interested in the history and remains of the quarries. In 1980 a footbridge across the Nant Gwernol ravine was opened giving access from Abergynolwyn village, and these days a number of booklets may be purchased from the railway giving details of guided walks and footpaths around the former quarry area, including two of the former inclines which may still be viewed.

Morfa Mawddach to Pwllheli

Barmouth railway bridge stretches for over half a mile across the mouth of the beautiful River Mawddach, and, after the payment

Barmouth Bridge, the pedestrians' way across. (Phillip Earnshaw)

Barmouth Bridge originally had a section that could be swung to allow the passage of ships up the River Mawddach. (Author)

of a small toll, a walk along its footpath beside the railway line is an unforgettable experience with magnificent inland views. It originally had a swing bridge section to allow the passage of ships up the river. Sometimes the bridge stands completely in water, the foundations being 120 ft below high water level, while at other times it is almost entirely exposed on the sand. Unfortunately in 1980 an inspection of the wooden pier foundations found evidence of serious damage caused by a type of wood-boring insect normally found only on ships. British Rail was forced to close the bridge and there was concern that closure would be permanent, both for Barmouth Bridge itself and for the whole line further north. However, funds have fortunately been found to strengthen the bridge and make it safe. For many years only diesel multiple units had been allowed across, and then at very low speeds but steam-hauled excursions returned to the Cambrian Coast in 2005 and railtours headed by heritage diesel-electric locomotives are also now able to reach Barmouth, Porthmadog or Pwllheli.

After passing Harlech, below its famous castle, the line crosses the Avon Glaslyn, burrows under the Ffestiniog Railway and enters Porthmadog where the station lies to the north-west of the town. The last 12 miles into Pwllheli is almost due west, passing Criccieth, where another castle juts right out into the sea, and the former junction with the Caernarfon line at Afon Wen. Stations were provided at Barmouth, Dyffryn (now Dyffryn Ardudwy), Pensarn (formerly Llanbedr & Pensarn), Harlech, Talsarnau, Penrhyndeudraeth, Minffordd (adjoining the Ffestiniog station), Porthmadog, Criccieth, Abererch and Pwllheli. Halts were added at Llanaber (1914), Talybont (1914), Talwrn Beach (now Pensarn, opened in 1923), Llandanwg (1929), Tygwyn (1927), Llandecwyn (1930), Black Rock (1923) and Penychain (now Butlins Penychain, 1933). Although the Caernarfon line junction at Avon Wen closed when that line ceased to operate in 1964, the other minor stations have fared better than those on the southern part of this route, with only Black Rock Halt, closed in 1976, no longer in operation.

The original terminus at Pwllheli was replaced in 1909 by a larger station situated west of the former and nearer to the centre of the town. Like many seaside resort termini, Pwllheli retained facilities into the 1970s way beyond those required for the basic six trains per day service it then had. The station had two platforms (at one time four) and there were two signal boxes, one to control the station area and one to control the goods yard. The inevitable rationalisation was made in the latter part of 1977; both signal boxes were abolished (one was moved to control operations at Minehead on the preserved West Somerset Railway as also, recently, has the old turntable) and one platform was closed, with a supermarket later built on its site.

In 1896 a 3 ft 6 inch gauge roadside tramway, horse drawn, was opened to take passengers further along the coast to Llanbedrog, a distance of around 4 miles. Buses replaced this service in 1927.

Nantlle Railway

The stories of the lines heading south from Caernarfon are somewhat complex and interwoven, but from a chronological point of view it is best to start with the Nantlle Railway. Authorised by an Act of 1825, the Nantlle Railway was up and running by 1828, taking slate and copper from mines and quarries in the Nantlle Valley to riverside quays in Caernarfon, close to the castle. Robert and George Stephenson were involved in its construction, the date indicating that this was shortly before they moved on to developing standard gauge passenger routes such as the Liverpool & Manchester. The line ran for 9 miles and was constructed at the unusual gauge of 3 ft 6 inches; this indicated a gauge chosen for its suitability to the traffic to be shipped and the local landscape; also that given its early date there were no other (standard or narrow gauge) lines to link up with. Running west from Nantlle to a station on the main road at Penygroes (where for a time a horse drawn bus operated a service south to Porthmadog), the line then turned sharply to the north as it descended to Caernarfon.

In 1857, plans were announced to build a link from Caernarfon to the coast between Pwllheli and Porthmadog, and this included conversion of much of the course of the Nantlle line to standard

Stone overbridge on the Nantlle Railway. The line ran on a different alignment to the later Afon Wen route at Dinas. (Author)

gauge. Once this line had been built, it would have made sense to convert the rest of the Nantlle to standard gauge, but only the section up to Nantlle station was ever widened. At the same time a new station at Penygroes was constructed a few hundred yards south west of the original, with a shorter link to Nantlle passing east from the south end of the new station. The line onto Caernarfon Quay also closed at this time, once a connection to the Bangor line had been constructed. Although most of the section north of Penygroes was built on the course of the Nantlle Railway, in places it took a slightly different course to reduce the level of curvature. This was particularly noticeable on the southern approach to Caernarfon from the junction with the Welsh Highland line at Dinas, where the Nantlle station at Bont Newydd was entirely bypassed.

The short branch from Penygroes to Nantlle closed to passengers in 1932, but the line into the quarries, still 3 ft 6 inches gauge, continued on into the nationalisation era, having the unique distinctions of being both the only line of that gauge and the only horse drawn line (there was nowhere from which to source suitable locomotives) ever to be operated by British Railways. The branch to Nantlle eventually closed in 1963.

Much of the trackbed between Nantlle and Penygroes was converted to a road, allowing trucks and tourists to avoid the winding streets of Nantlle itself. More remnants can be found on the section north to Caernarfon, where the later standard gauge line took a slightly different course. A tunnel with adjacent cuttings (in remarkably good condition) may still be viewed close to the former junction with the Welsh Highland Railway at Dinas, whilst near Bont Newydd eagle-eyed passengers on the landward side of WHR carriages may be able to spot the old Nantlle embankment, and the arch of the original river bridge, which still stands over 130 years after being abandoned.

Afon Wen to Caernarfon

Originally promoted by the Caernarfonshire Railway, this route opened for business in September 1867, having in effect bought out the Nantlle Railway. Questions were asked about how much care had been taken in its construction; the line only passed its line inspection at the third attempt. By 1870 this route had become part of the LNWR, and hence after nationalisation passed to the London Midland region of British Railways.

The Afon Wen Line was at its busiest in the summer months after the Second World War, following the opening of a holiday camp by Butlins at Penychain; the most direct route from the North of England being via the North Wales Coast line and then south through Bangor and Caernarfon. Heading north from the isolated junction station at Afon Wen, stations were provided at Chwilog, Brynkir, Penygroes, Groeslon and Llanwnda, with further ones added shortly after at Llangybi (1870), Ynys (1871), Pant Glas (1871) and Dinas Junction (1877).

Afon Wen to Caernarfon line, Brynkir station. (Leslie Oppitz Collection)

Dinas (Junction), serving little purpose after the Welsh Highland ceased operation, closed in 1951 and Pant Glas followed in 1957, but the line continued to be useful for freight (mostly slate) carriage up until the early 1960s. When that traffic ceased it was clearly vulnerable to the 'rationalisation' plans of the time, and closure took place in December 1964.

The trackbed was purchased by Caernarfonshire County Council (later Gwynedd) in 1968, not initially for the purposes of creating a trail, but more to use some short stretches for road improvements (which they did to some extent in Caernarfon itself) and then to sell on what they did not need. The central section, from Llanwnda to a point a mile or so north of Pant Glas station, was acquired by the building firm McAlpines, who used the formation to create a road for lorries to bring aggregate to the construction site for a hydro-electric scheme at Dinorwig. By the time this was completed, in 1983, the formation reverted to local authority ownership and the possibility of creating an official path on the line was now being proposed. This was finally completed as far south as Brynkir, most of the section between

Afon Wen to Caernarfon line, Llanwnda station (Leslie Oppitz Collection)

here and Afon Wen having been sold off for private use, but this still leaves over 12 miles of trackbed open for walking and exploration. At Brynkir overgrown platforms remain, and fine views may be had of the distant mountains of Snowdonia to the east as you enjoy a grassy and natural surface to walk on. At Pant Glas a wooden platform face may just be seen, hidden beneath brambles, but unfortunately the station buildings at Penygroes and Llanwnda were destroyed by McAlpines during their tenure of this part of the line. Penygroes, in particular, was a fine structure; a two storey brick building delicately constructed in a decorative bond. The former truck road here provides a firm, all-weather surface, ideal for cycling, and a purpose built path continues on from where the contractor's track left the formation. From Dinas Junction into Caernarfon, the formation is now shared with the Welsh Highland Railway, and about ¾ mile south of Caernarfon passes across a short but lofty viaduct over the Afon Seiont. This viaduct may look unexceptional from the trackbed but is most impressive if you can clamber down to view it from below.

10
Railways to Blaenau Ffestiniog

Festiniog Railway
Blaenau Ffestiniog to Llandudno Junction
Bala to Blaenau Ffestiniog
The Llechwydd Slate Caverns

The original station at Blaenau Ffestiniog. (Leslie Oppitz Collection)

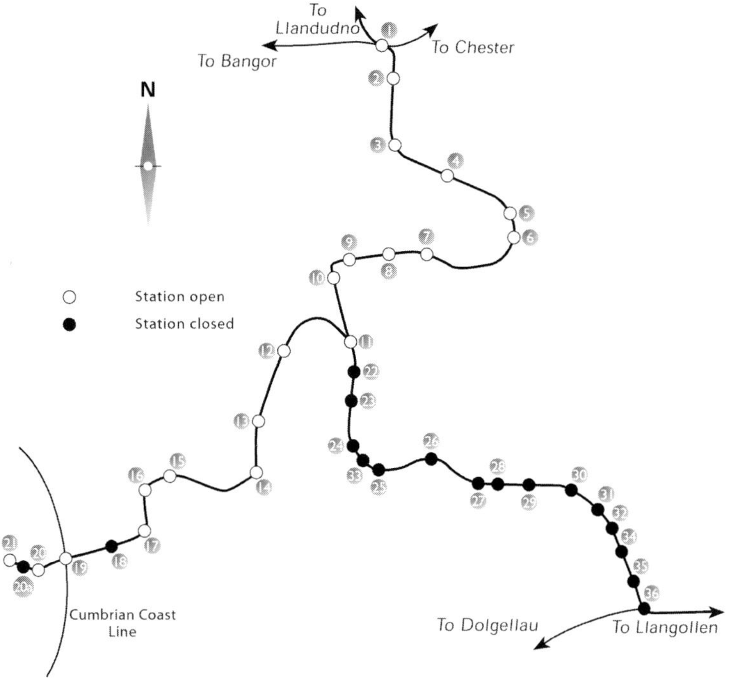

1. Llandudno Junction
2. Glan Conwy
3. Tal-y-cafn
4. Dolgarrog
5. North Llanrwst
6. Llanrwst
7. Betws-y-Coed
8. Pont-y-Pant
9. Dolwyddelan
10. Roman Bridge
11. Blaenau Ffestiniog
12. Tan-y-grisiau
13. Llyn Ystradau
14. Dduallt
15. Tan-y-bwlch
16. Plas Halt
17. Penrhyndeudraeth
18. Pen-y-bryn Halt
19. Minffordd
20. Boston Lodge
20a. Pen Cob Halt
21. Portmadog Harbour
22. Manod
23. Teigi Halt
24. Ffestiniog
25. Trawsfynydd Lake Halt
26. Trawsfynydd
27. Llafar Halt
28. Bryncelynog Halt
29. Cwm Prysor
30. Arenig
31. Capel Celyn Halt
32. Tyddyn Bridge Halt
33. Maentwrog Road
34. Frongoch
35. Bala
36. Bala Junction

The first railway to reach Blaenau Ffestiniog was the Festiniog, which provided the shortest route to the sea for the outward transfer of slate. Given the scale (slates were the first choice of roofing materials for all pitched roof buildings well into the 20th century) and profitability of this traffic, both the LNWR and GWR were also keen to build lines into the area to tap into this trade. On completion of the Conwy Valley line, the LNWR built a station to the north of the town, which was used until 1982. At that time the present, more centrally located, station, shared by the Conwy Valley and Festiniog lines, opened on the site of the GWR station which was served via Bala. The former LNWR station still has its building, boarded up but intact, together with a now partly gorse-covered platform and the remains of metal nameboards, next to the old goods yard.

The former LNWR station at Blaenau Ffestiniog. (Author)

A gorse-covered platform with the remains of a nameboard still stretches out towards the mountains of slate at Blaenau. (Author)

Festiniog Railway

Perhaps the line with the proudest history of all, the Festiniog Railway Company is the world's oldest independent railway company, established by an Act of Parliament passed in 1832. A gauge of 1 ft 11 inches was chosen as this was already being used for the tramways in the quarries.

By the early 1820s, the town's founder Mr W. Madocks had reclaimed land and built an embankment, the Cob, across the estuary of the River Glaslyn at Porthmadog thus creating a harbour, which enabled ships of some size to dock and transport the slate away down the coast.

Opening in April 1836, the Festiniog was first worked by horses hauling empty wagons from Porthmadog back up to the quarries, then returning in dandy carts to the harbour. There were also at this time two inclines south of Tan-y-grisiau. By 1856 horses were proving inadequate and consideration was given to the possible use of locomotive power on the narrow gauge line. In 1863 the first steam locomotives, named *The Princess* and *Mountaineer*, arrived and following successful trials entered into service in October. At the same time permission was given to run passenger trains, largely for the benefit of the quarrymen who could then travel to work from the villages and farmsteads close to the line.

By the 1860s these early locomotives were found to be insufficiently powerful for the volume of traffic they were required to haul. The search for a more powerful engine resulted in the appointment of Robert Fairlie, who designed a double-bogie engine, effectively two locomotives joined back-to-back. This design proved so successful that these engines remain in regular use today, with similar designs in use on steeply graded narrow gauge lines in many other parts of the world.

Competition for the Festiniog started to grow by the 1870s, when first the LNWR and later the GWR built their own lines to Blaenau. However, the Festiniog continued to thrive; by the 1920s tourist traffic had started to grow and had become nearly as important as the slate carriage.

By 1930, however, the Festiniog was running at a loss and a decision was taken to cease winter passenger services in October

Festiniog Railway, at Minffordd. (Leslie Oppitz Collection)

Tan-y-bwlch station, with its long 'S' shaped island platform, remains a most delightful and photogenic location. (Author)

of that year, whilst the Second World War put an end to the tourist trains. Slate traffic also declined, the last shipload leaving the harbour in 1945. There were now alternative roofing materials available, and in any case there was an acute lack of labour available to work the quarries. By August 1946 the line had closed completely.

Following the successful rebirth of the Talyllyn (see Chapter 9), a group of enthusiasts were brought together to see if something similar could be done for the Festiniog. Initially volunteers were only able to cut back and re-lay the overgrown track, repair locomotives and carriages, and to attend to the buildings that had been left neglected for many years. However, in July 1955, passenger services were resumed between Porthmadog and Boston Lodge, reaching Minffordd the following year with gradual extensions completed after that.

A major challenge arose when construction of a reservoir and a pumped storage scheme near Tan-y-grisiau, led to part of the line being submerged. This left an unusable section of track between Dduallt and Tan-y-grisiau, including the 600 yard Moelwyn Tunnel, which had to be abandoned, though the top of the northern portal of the original tunnel occasionally re-emerges from its watery grave when periods of prolonged dry weather empty the reservoir. The railway company was forced to build a

Ffestiniog Railway; Fairlie engine 'David Lloyd George' at Tan-y-bwlch. (Author)

completely new section of track starting from Dduallt at a higher level by means of a spiral, and with a shorter tunnel at Moelwyn. Reopening of the full line, including a new interchange station with the standard gauge line at Blaenau, took place in May 1982 and the popularity of a ride on the Ffestiniog shows no sign of declining.

Those interested in old lines may wish to combine a trip on the Ffestiniog with some exploration of the tramways that branched away from the 'main line'. The Rhiwbach tramway was the longest of the feeders to the Ffestiniog; from Blaenau it rose by the use of three long inclines and then ran across the moors to a number of different quarries. Another line ran from Tan-y-grisiau up Cwm Orthin to Conglog and Rhosydd Quarries via two steep inclines.

Blaenau Ffestiniog to Llandudno Junction

Opened in stages, first to Llanrwst by 1863, and then reaching Betws-y-coed by 1868, the LNWR dithered about attempting to reach Blaenau. Fearful of the cost and engineering requirements, particularly in view of the need for a long tunnel under Moel Dyrnogydd, they were urged on by the slate owners whose market was rapidly expanding. At one stage the LNWR considered a narrow gauge line, but in 1872 made the decision to construct a standard gauge tunnel. However, it was not until 1879 that the line south of Betws to a temporary station at Dinas, just south of the tunnel, was opened. The LNWR station (later given the affix 'north') in Blaenau Ffestiniog finally opened on 1st April 1881. At 2 miles and 338 yards, Ffestiniog Tunnel was and still is the longest single track tunnel to be built anywhere in Britain. At 28 miles, with a journey time of around an hour, the Conwy Valley line provides one of the most spectacular journeys imaginable. The tourist hot spot of Betws-y-coed has a most remarkable station, a single platform of apparently infinite length, completely covered at its northern end in nettles and brambles as

Blaenau Ffestiniog station today; standard and narrow gauge at the same location. (Author)

Betws-y-coed station, on the Conwy Valley line, today. (Author)

it heads into the distance around a curve. The usable area of the platform has a whole street of shops and restaurants backing onto it, with a variety of seating on the platform itself. For a while there was a second platform, with faces on both sides, but this has long gone, and on its former site is a miniature railway with a small museum. Climbing through the valley at gradients steeper than 1 in 50, the branch then passes the superb 12th century Dolwyddelan Castle and the high peaks of Snowdonia, before entering the heart of the mountain to emerge some minutes later in the stunning and unique industrial landscape of Blaenau Ffestiniog.

The line might well have closed in the 1960s had it not been needed for a route to Trawsfynydd Power Station (see below), as all other freight traffic had ceased by 1968 and passenger receipts at the time did not get anywhere near to paying the costs of keeping the line open. Tourist traffic gradually increased and was much boosted by the return of the Ffestiniog Railway to Blaenau. Although prone to flooding and sometimes closed for quite lengthy periods for that reason, the Conwy Valley line's future now appears secure. A daily service of six trains each way is currently in operation.

Bala to Blaenau Ffestiniog

Regarded by many who travelled on it as being even more spectacular than the Conwy Valley route, the GWR Bala and Festiniog line opened on 1st November 1882. Climbing from Bala to a summit of 1,278 ft at Cwm Prysor the line passed Arenig station where sidings served modest slate quarries. The descent involved a horseshoe curve around the apex of the Cynfal Valley and a spectacular viaduct at Cwm Prysor, nine arches carrying the line over 100 ft above the infant Afon Prysor. The line twice served major installations at Trawsfynydd, close to the lake of that name. In 1903 an artillery camp was opened, an extensive troop yard having its own platforms for the military traffic, whilst in the 1960s a nuclear power station was built here, though this was never served directly from Bala.

Bala Town station on the Blaenau route. (Leslie Oppitz Collection)

The Bala route closed in 1961, partly as a result of the need for a section of the line to be flooded for a new reservoir at Llyn Celyn in the Treweryn Valley, though construction of a diversionary route at a slightly higher level would not have been difficult and powers for purchase of the necessary land were obtained. Having always remained separate from the LNWR, a link line was built in 1964 to allow the nuclear traffic to travel down the Conwy Valley then traverse 5 miles of the old GWR line to reach the power station.

For a few years from 1989, as part of a plan to encourage more visitors to the power station, it was decided to extend some of the valley line's Sunday services to a new platform at Maentwrog Road. The platform was paid for by the CEGB and the service ran for eight weeks during the summer months. A bus connection to the power station met prospective visitors. Unfortunately this service ceased when the power station closed in 1994, though the line was at that time kept open for occasional traffic associated with its maintenance. The final train to Trawsfynydd ran on 17th October 1998. The trackbed is protected from development in case the line is ever required again, and rusty tracks still head out of the south side of Blaenau.

The eastern end of the former Bala line lends itself well to exploration. Two sections are now open to the public as footpaths; firstly a one mile segment from Bryn Ifan to Arenig. The 4½ mile

Trawsfynydd station on the former GWR Bala line. (Leslie Oppitz Collection)

Trawsfynydd today; a rusty track still runs through the site somewhere under the bushes! (Author)

section from Cwm Prysor to Glanllafar, passing remote countryside once protected with snow fences in sections and crossing the still spectacular Cwm Prysor Viaduct, is as good a railway walk as you will find anywhere in Britain. A one mile extension of this route westwards to Trawsfynydd should be completed by 2008.

Of other remains, the former station at Trawsfynydd has been beautifully restored as a private dwelling, complete with a superbly manicured lawn in between the platforms. Close by, the site of the former artillery camp platform is marked by fence posts made up of surplus GWR broad gauge rail. The station houses at Cwm Prysor and Maentwrog Road remain in residential use whilst Frongoch station has also survived under private occupation, complete with its signal box in its original position on the platform. Arenig was not so fortunate, its site having been completely cleared after at one stage being used as a yard for a quarry merchant. Similarly there are minimal remains at the sites of both Manod and Ffestiniog stations, though here the rusty rails remain *in situ*.

The Llechwydd Slate Caverns

The slate caverns which had roofed the houses and industrial buildings of Britain and Europe were a mystery to all but the miners who made them, until 1972, when a half-mile level section of the Miners' Tramway was opened to the world. This now provides the perfect opportunity for visitors to experience the caverns and the work that went on within them. Boarding a train in a corner of the original slate slabbing mill of 1852, travellers now ride into an 1846 tunnel, hauled by a battery powered locomotive. Entering through the side of the mountain this journey into the early Victorian past remains on the level, and traverses some spectacular caverns. To reach the 'Deep Mine', visitors descend in specially designed 3 ft gauge cars on Britain's steepest passenger railway, with a gradient of 1 in 1.8, to make the Deep Mine tour.

11
Railways to Llanberis

Padarn Railway
Caernarfon to Llanberis
Llanberis Lake Railway
Snowdon Mountain Railway

Llanberis terminus, in the shadows of Snowdonia. (Lens of Sutton)

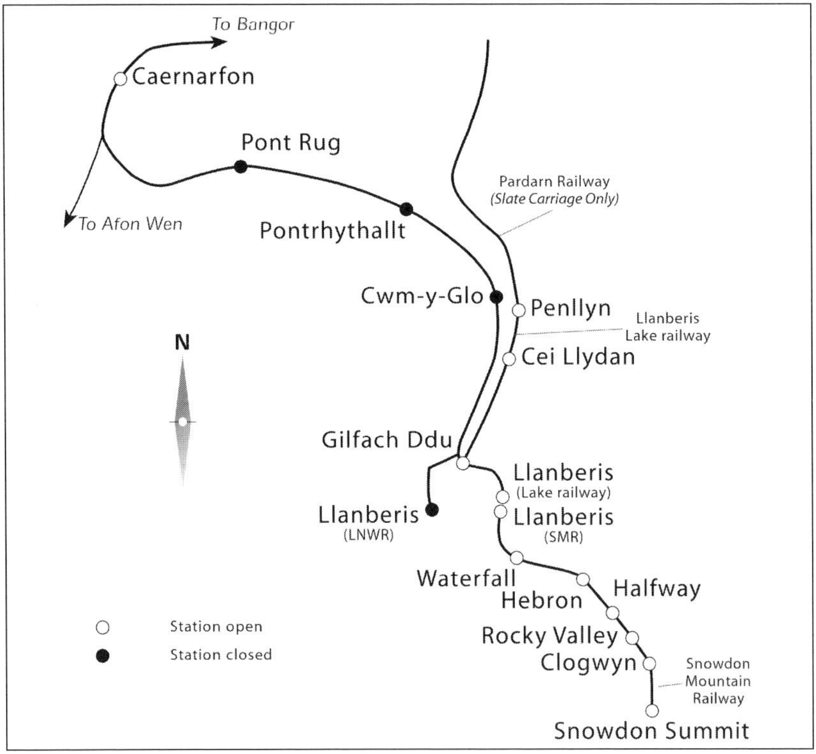

Padarn Railway

On the north bank of the Llyn Padarn a 2 ft gauge primitive railway was opened in 1824 from Allt Ddu (near Deiniolen) to a quay at Port Dinorwic. Constructed by the quarry owners, it is recorded that by 1840 over 60 tons of slate were carried daily down the line, in trains worked by a mixture of animal haulage and gravity. This tramway was, however, poorly engineered and an alternative route with a higher carrying capacity was constructed along a comparatively level route from Llanberis. This route later became the 4 ft gauge Padarn Railway, on which steam locomotives hauled both slate trains and workmen's trains for the quarrymen, though there was never an official passenger service along this line.

Quayside at Port Dinorwic (Y Felenheli), terminus of the Padarn Railway. (Author)

Inside the quarries, slate was cut from the mountain in a series of huge galleries, each one connected to the one below by a sloping path, down which the slates were slid on sledges. Gradually this arrangement was replaced by a system of 2 ft gauge railways, using inclines between the levels. At first these were horse drawn, but by 1870 tiny locomotives were taking their place. After the Second World War, diesel locomotives rapidly took over a lot of the quarry work, and gradually the steam locomotives were sold off to other lines or to private collectors.

The Padarn Railway was closed in October 1961, and soon afterwards the rails were removed and the engines and rolling stock broken up for scrap. Other than the section used for the lake railway, much of the route of the railway was abandoned to nature and rapidly became overgrown. A short section of line south of Pontrhythallt has been converted to a public footpath, and sections of trackbed may be seen north of Saron, but there is no official access to the majority of the remains of the formation.

Caernarfon to Llanberis

The second railway to pass along the shores of Llyn Padarn, this line was inaugurated by a local company, the Caernarvon & Llanberis, opening in 1869 from Llanberis to a temporary station

Timber bridge over River Rug on the Llanberis branch. (Author)

known as Morfa on the outskirts of Caernarfon. Although originally envisaged as an outlet for slate quarried at Llanberis, the Padarn Railway always maintained a monopoly of this traffic, and so the LNWR had to make do with fairly meagre local traffic, excursions and some general goods work. Originally there was just one intermediate station, at Cwm-y-glo, close to a short tunnel of 106 yards in length, but two others were added later; Pontrhythallt (shortly after opening, in 1869) and Pont Rug (1880). The line suffered early closure to regular passenger services, in September 1930. However, it remained popular with day trippers and to this end an additional stop, known as Padarn Halt, was opened in November 1936, at a lakeside location a mile or so to the north-west of Llanberis. Excursion trains remained popular well into the 1950s, but eventually died away and after freight traffic ceased the line closed completely in September 1964.

The Caernarfon end was quickly built on after closure and the approach to Llanberis was used as a route for a bypass for the small town. At Cwm-y-glo part of the formation, including the old tunnel, has been incorporated into the Lon Las Peris Trail. Other sections of the trackbed can still be traced, but they are largely in private hands. What is left has also been fragmented by the removal of a number of bridges over the adjacent rivers, though one fine timber example survives to the east of Llanrug.

Llanberis Lake Railway

Promoters wanting to cash in on the 1970s 'Narrow Gauge Mania' in North Wales found an ideal location along the northern banks

The new terminus of the Lake Railway at Llanberis. (Author)

of the Llyn Padarn, the erstwhile Padarn Railway providing the route beside the lake with the old quarries providing some of the fittings. Construction started in the autumn of 1970, when the dense growth of trees, gorse, heather and brambles was removed from the route, and the new track put down, using rails salvaged from the quarry. The line was opened in July 1971, when visitors were able to travel to Cei Llydan; and was extended further to Penllyn in 1972. For a few years from 1974 the railway had a year-round freight-carrying role; it was used by the CEGB for laying underground cables associated with a hydro-electric scheme at the lake. Use of the railway in this way avoided the construction of roadways and tracks for the heavy lorries that would otherwise have been required, and thus disturbance to the beautiful surroundings was kept to a minimum.

In 2002, after many years of planning, an ambitious project to link the railway to Llanberis village got under way, including the laying of half a mile of track, two level crossings, the construction of a large river bridge and the building of a new terminal station. This is situated just across the road from the Snowdon Mountain Railway and thus forms a convenient link between the two lines. The new extension was opened to the public in June 2003.

Snowdon Mountain Railway

Ever since 1869, when tourists keen to enjoy the delights of Snowdon started to arrive on the newly opened branch line to

Llanberis, proposals were being made for a railway to take them to the summit of the highest mountain in Wales. The local landowner George William Duff Assherton Smith initially thought that a railway would spoil the scenery and turned down every promoter for the next twenty years but then a rival plan to build a railway to the summit of Snowdon, from Rhys Ddu station on the Welsh Highland line (at that time a North Wales Narrow Gauge Railways line) on the other side of the mountain, brought fears that Llanberis would lose its tourist trade forever. With this in mind Assherton Smith changed his mind and authorised construction of a railway. Building began in 1894 and a grand opening took place on 6th April 1896.

The day was marred, however, by an accident involving the locomotive *Ladas*, which derailed at Colwyn and fell into a ravine. Although the coaches were brought safely to a halt, a man died after jumping from the train in panic.

The line was built at a gauge of 2 ft 7½ inches, and in just over 4½ miles climbs over 3,000 ft at a maximum gradient of 1 in 5½. It is single track, with three intermediate passing loops, and each train nowadays consists of just one carriage and its engine. Much of the technology used by the SMR is taken from similar lines in

A 1960s' view of the Snowdon Mountain Railway's Llanberis station. (Leslie Oppitz Collection)

Switzerland, as are the locomotives themselves, and is used nowhere else in Britain. Designed by a German engineer, Dr Roman Abt, smooth and constant operation when tackling the steep gradients is achieved by a double racked rail, one rack slightly offset with respect to the other, used with a rotating toothed pinion. The pinion is mounted underneath the locomotive and guarantees the locomotive does not lose grip on the mountain. Unique to rack railways, the locomotive always pushes the carriage up the mountain and, for safety reasons, is never coupled to the train. The carriage has its own set of brakes that brings it to a standstill if it should ever disengage from the locomotive. In recent years a fine exhibition on the line has been put together at the Llanberis terminus.

Snowdon Mountain Railway wheel and axle set, showing the offset rack system which enables the locomotives to ascend steep gradients. (Author)

Snowdon Mountain Railway locomotive No 12, 'George', ready to propel its coach to the summit. (Author)

12
Lines around Caernarfon and Bangor

Caernarfon
Welsh Highland Railway
Tramways of the Welsh Highland Railway
Bangor to Caernarfon
Penrhyn Railway and Port Penrhyn branch
Bangor to Bethesda

Carnarvon (Caernarfon) station. (Lens of Sutton)

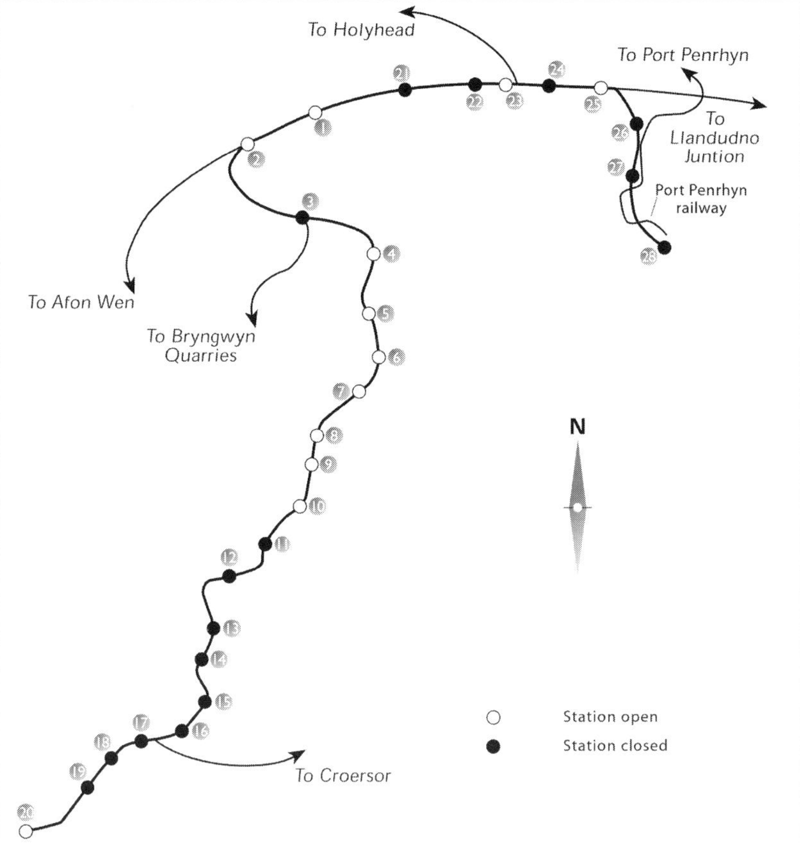

1. Caernarfon
2. Dinas Junction
3. Tryfan Junction
4. Waunfawr
5. Betws Garmon
6. Salem
7. Plas-y-nant
8. Quellyn
9. Quellyn Lake
10. Rhyd Ddu
11. Pitt's Head
12. Hafod Ruffydd
13. Beddgelert
14. Aberglaslyn
15. Hafod-y-llyn
16. Haford Garregog
17. Croesor Junction
18. Ynysfor
19. Pont Croesor
20. Porthmadog (WHR)
21. Griffiths Crossing Halt
22. Port Dinorwic
23. Treborth
24. Menai Bridge
25. Bangor
26. Felin Hen Halt
27. Tregarth
28. Bethesda

Caernarfon

Originally a fortification, the name Caernarfon (anglicised to Caernarvon or Carnavon) comes from Y Gear yen Afon, the Fort of Arvin. Fought over in the Middle Ages because of its strategic location, Caernarfon is dominated by its castle, so impressive and intact from the outside, but somewhat ruined on the inside. It was built by Edward I of England, who took it upon himself to 'invest' members of his family as 'Princes of Wales' and the castle is consequently seen by some as a symbol of English domination.

The first railway to arrive was the Nantlle, in 1828, reaching the harbour area, followed by its successor, the Caernarfonshire, whose first terminus was south of the River Seiont at Pant. With the line from Bangor terminating at the north of the town and the Llanberis line terminating at a station called Morfa, close to the Seiont, there were at one stage three unconnected stations within a mile and a half of each other. The solution was a linking line from the harbour area, passing under the town centre by means of a 163 yard tunnel, and a climb at 1 in 40 through a cutting to reach what by now was the LNWR station on the Bangor line. Opening was in July 1870 to goods and January 1871 to freight, with the two temporary stations to the south then closing.

Welsh Highland Railway

Opened as a single identity as late as 1923, the Welsh Highland Railway was formed by the merger of several much older railways: the Croesor Tramway, the North Wales Narrow Gauge Railways, and the Portmadoc, Beddgelert & South Snowdon Railway.

The Croesor Tramway had been opened in 1863. It was purely horse drawn, carrying mainly slate traffic and extended from Porthmadog to the slate mines surrounding Croesor village. This tramway crossed the Cambrian Coast main line railway (originally the Aberystwyth & Welch Coast Railway) on the level to reach the town and harbour at Porthmadog.

The North Wales Narrow Gauge Railways (NWNGR) had been opened in 1877. The line ran southwards from Dinas Junction, near Caernarfon. As its name implies, it had been intended to be one of a network of narrow gauge lines through western Snowdonia, most of which never came to fruition.

Plans were made from as early as 1872 to link the two tramways by driving a line through Beddgelert, but it was not until the summer of 1923 that the Welsh Highland Railway was able to pull its first passenger trains through the mountains. It operated very much in partnership with the neighbouring Ffestiniog Railway, with which it shared a gauge and some rolling stock. However, it was never a commercial success; a receiver was appointed in 1927, and closure came ten years later, with the track lifted for scrap in 1941.

After many years of planning and discussion, in 1996 a new company called the Welsh Highland Light Railway (WHLR) was formed, in association with the Ffestiniog Railway, to lead reconstruction of the route. Earlier, in December 1995, planning permission had been granted for building a new link from Caernarfon to Dinas, and with the WHLR having been approved by the Millennium Commission for a major grant towards rebuilding from Caernarfon to Rhyd Ddu significant progress could then be made. Starting near the quayside at the ancient port of Caernarfon, the route climbs on the old standard gauge trackbed to the former junction with the original WHR at Dinas Junction, the terminus of the old WHR, which happily is now a railway depot and station once again. Both the original NWNGR/WHR station building, and the goods shed remain. On departure for Waunfawr the line then curves southwards, on a slightly different formation to the original, and joins the WHR trackbed proper on the site of the old yard. From here to the current (2008) terminus at Rhyd Ddu, the line takes a somewhat circuitous route, climbing almost the whole way. Extending the line through Beddgelert involved the ending of public access to what had been a popular and spectacular railway walk, passing through three tunnels as the line crept through the narrow Aberglaslyn Pass. There was some disappointment amongst locals that the railway authorities chose to close off access here some years before starting to rebuild the line. Reconstruction of the railway eventually began in 2006 and by April 2008 rails had been laid on the bridge over the River Glaslyn which is shared with the B4410 road, little more than a mile away from the northern terminus of the current operation from Porthmadog (WHR) station. Discussions are ongoing about possibly eventually reinstating the railway through Porthmadog to reach the harbour and once again link with the Ffestiniog Railway.

Tramways of the Welsh Highland Railway

The Welsh Highland, partly due to its piecemeal history, still has a number of tramways and minor routes branching off which are available for exploration. The Bryngwyn branch was perhaps the most important. From Tryfan Junction, between Dinas and Waunfawr, the line proceeded up an incline to a point known as 'Drumhead', where the tramways from the quarries converged. Rising just 245 ft in half a mile, the Bryngwyn incline is a good deal less steep than many of its kind. Much of the incline remains visible; particularly its less overgrown upper section. From Drumhead, a number of routes can still be viewed; the two mile long Alexandra Quarry Tramway being perhaps the most striking. The line was built in 1876 (open by December); part of it seems to have fallen out of use after the various quarries came under common management after the First World War. Later on in this period Alexandra was worked via a tunnel connection with Moel Tryfan Quarry. The tramway is thought to have been lifted by 1939. Other tramways reached quarries at Moel Tryfan and Braich. It is a shame that at present there is no easy access by rail to this area; the provision of a halt at Tryfan would make life a lot easier for the explorer of these old routes.

South of Waunfawr, a tramway ran to Hafod-y-wern slate quarry (closed mid-1920s), which more recently has been a source of the crushed slate waste laid on the WHR trackbed prior to ballasting. Its formation is largely intact. Further back towards Waunfawr, another sharply-curved tramway crossed the River

Gwyrfai to serve the Treflan and Garreg Fawr slate quarries and an iron ore mine, half a mile from the main line. The dates of this tramway are not entirely clear; it is thought to have been opened in about 1901–2 and appears to have operated for about ten years, as a 1916 Ordnance Survey map shows just the course of the tramway without a rail connection.

Further south, the line of the westernmost section of the former Croesor Tramway may still be viewed, reaching a quarry at New Rhosydd via a spectacular route involving a number of inclines. Much of this route is, however, on private land, and permission to view the remains should therefore be obtained from the landowners.

Bangor to Caernarfon

Following the opening of the Holyhead line, a branch to Caernarfon was an obvious priority but first plans were to go only as far as Port Dinorwic (Y Felenheli), where a link could be made with the slate-carrying Padarn Railway. However, the Bangor & Carnarvon Railway gained authority to construct a line to Caernarfon, and a branch (or, more accurately, a long siding) to Port Dinorwic opened in stages between March and August 1852. Much of the land was flat and required little in the way of earthworks other than the 497 yard Vaynol Tunnel. Originally there was just one intermediate station, at Port Dinorwic, but a station was opened in 1855 at Treborth,

Port Dinorwic station, between Bangor and Caernarfon. (Leslie Oppitz Collection)

just south of the Britannia Bridge and a halt opened at Griffiths Crossing, a couple of miles north-east of Caernarfon. The sections between Menai Bridge and Treborth and Port Dinorwic to Caernarfon were doubled in 1872, reflecting the heavy use of this line. The remaining section with a second tunnel at Vaynol and a resiting southwards of Port Dinorwic station, followed in 1874.

Whilst the little-used Griffiths Crossing halt closed in 1937 and Treborth station followed in 1959, the first section to cease operation was the branch to the harbour at Port Dinorwic, closing at the same time as the Padarn Railway in October 1961. Attempts were made to reduce costs by singling the line after Caernarfon had become a terminus in 1966, but this failed to make sufficient savings. The line closed to passengers in January 1970 but had the unusual distinction of being reopened temporarily as an emergency terminus for freightliner traffic whilst the Britannia Bridge was being rebuilt. Final closure took place in February 1972 with the track lifted later that year.

The section between Caernarfon and Griffiths Crossing, including Caernarfon Tunnel, was purchased by the council and quickly converted to a new bypass road, but much of the line is now an official footpath and cycleway. The station building at Port Dinorwic remains intact, albeit with major refurbishment. All remains on the quayside at Port Dinorwic were destroyed by the construction of a new marina.

Port Dinorwic station undergoing refurbishment in 2008. (Author)

Penrhyn Railway and Port Penrhyn branch

The 1 ft, 10¾ inch gauge Penrhyn Railway is thought to be the earliest narrow gauge line of any length in North Wales. Opened in 1801 it was designed to be horse-drawn, built in level stretches separated by inclined planes at intervals to gain height rather in the manner of a canal. It stretched for over 6 miles from slate quarries at Bethesda to the quayside at Port Penrhyn. Following the opening of the Chester & Holyhead, the Port Penrhyn branch, 1½ miles in length, was built from the main line west of Llandegai Tunnel to reach the harbour. This line was privately-owned and ran for its whole length through the estate of Lord Penrhyn. Conversion of the Penrhyn to locomotive haulage and abolition of the inclined planes by use of a slightly amended route took place as late as 1877 but even so, for over 80 years, tiny locomotives could be seen hauling slate down to the harbour and returning up the gradient with the empties. By 1872 the LNWR was taking an interest in the line with regard to conversion to a standard gauge line carrying passengers, but the Penrhyn was profitable as it was and never ran a public passenger service. There were, though, some unofficial services for quarry employees and other workmen; these apparently finished in February 1951. The Penrhyn continued on until July 1962 when a sharp decline in traffic brought its closure. The Port Penrhyn branch followed shortly after, closing in March 1963. By this time the Penrhyn estate had been passed to the National

Much of the Penrhyn Railway line is now a popular footpath and cycleway. (Author)

Trust, and this helped the preservation of much of the old line. The section from Bangor south as far as Glasinfryn is now designated an official path and is popular with both walkers and cyclists.

Bangor to Bethesda

Having had their approaches to the Penrhyn owners rebuffed, and with local people still demanding a passenger service, the LNWR finally took action and an Act of Parliament authorising a standard gauge line to Bethesda was passed in August 1880. Opening in July 1884 to passengers, the line was difficult to squeeze into a narrow valley which already had one railway, crossing the Penrhyn three times and requiring a 297-yard tunnel at Tregarth. As well as the terminus, a halt was constructed at Felin Hen and a station provided at Tregarth, west of the tunnel. Without any slate traffic the line could never hope to be profitable and, by 1908, auto trains had replaced conventional locomotive and carriage arrangements. Closure to regular passengers came in December 1951, though excursion trains and goods traffic enabled the line to linger on until complete closure in July 1962. Little of this line has survived, though a short section in Tregarth is used as a footpath and as part of a playing field, while in Bethesda itself the formation has been obliterated by the A5 trunk road running through. The south portal of Tregarth Tunnel is open, but access is impossible as the adjacent cutting is completely waterlogged.

Bethesda branch; the remains of Felin Hen station. (Leslie Oppitz Collection)

BIBLIOGRAPHY

The following books are recommended for further reading; many are now out of print but can often be obtained via secondhand booksellers.

Baughan, Peter *A Regional History of the Railways of Great Britain, Volume 1: North and Mid Wales* (David & Charles)
Baxter, Bertram *Stone Blocks and Iron Roads* (Tramroads) (David & Charles)
Christiansen, Rex *Forgotten Railways: North & Mid Wales* (David & Charles)
Cobb, Colonel Michael H. *The Railways of Great Britain: A Historical Atlas* (Ian Allan Publishing)
Cockman, F.G. *Discovering Lost Railways* and *Discovering Preserved Railways* (Hire Publications)
Cozens, Lewis, Kidner, R.W. & Poole, Brian *The Mawddwy, Van & Kerry Branches* (Oakwood Press)
Croft, D.J. *A Survey of Seaside Miniature Railways* (Oakwood Press)
Hendry, Dr R.P. & Hendry, R.P. *An Historical Survey of Selected LMS Stations* (OPC)
Jones, Geraint I.L. *Anglesey Railways* (Carreg-Gwalch)
Kidner, R.W. *The Cambrian Railways* (Oakwood Press)
Oppitz, Leslie *Lost Railways of Shropshire* and *Lost Railways of Cheshire* (Countryside Books)
Owen-Jones, Stuart *Railways of Wales* (National Museums and Galleries of Wales)
Shannon, Paul & Hillier, John *British Railways Past and Present: Cheshire & North Wales* (Past and Present Publishing Ltd)
Vinter, Jeff *Railway Walks: Wales* (Alan Sutton Publishing)
Welbourn, Nigel *Lost Lines: British Narrow Gauge* (Ian Allan Publishing)
Great Western Railway Timetables October 1947 (Oxford Publishing Company)

INDEX